North Country Captives

NORTH COUNTRY CAPTIVES

Selected Narratives of Indian Captivity from
Vermont and New Hampshire

compiled and with an introduction by
Colin G. Calloway

UNIVERSITY PRESS OF NEW ENGLAND
Hanover and London

UNIVERSITY PRESS OF NEW ENGLAND
publishes books under its own imprint and
is the publisher for Brandeis University Press,
Dartmouth College, Middlebury College Press,
University of New Hampshire, Tufts University,
and Wesleyan University Press.

University Press of New England, Hanover, NH 03755
© 1992 by University Press of New England
Printed in the United States of America   5 4 3 2

Library of Congress Cataloging-in-Publication Data
North Country captives : selected narratives of Indian
captivity from Vermont and New Hampshire / [edited]
with an introduction by Colin G. Calloway.
            p. cm.
Includes bibliographical references (p.   ).
ISBN 0–87451–582–3 (pa)
1. Indians of North America—Vermont—
Captivities. 2. Indians of North America—New
Hampshire—Captivities. 3. Indians of North
America—Vermont—History. 4. Indians of North
America—New Hampshire—History. 5. Frontier
and pioneer life—Vermont. 6. Frontier and pioneer
life—New Hampshire. I. Calloway, Colin G. (Colin
Gordon), 1953– .
E78.V5N67 1992
974.2'00497—dc20   91–50810

Contents

Introduction
vii

Map of the North Country
xiii

A Narrative of the Captivity of Nehemiah How
(Putney, Vermont), 1745
1

The Captivity of Mary Fowler
(Hopkinton, New Hampshire), 1746
13

The Captivity of Isabella McCoy
(Epsom, New Hampshire), 1747
17

Journals of Captain Phineas Stevens
(Fort Number Four, New Hampshire),
1749 and *1752*
22

A Narrative of the Captivity of Mrs. Johnson
(Charlestown, New Hampshire), 1754,
with the deposition of James Johnson, *1757*
45

The Captivity and Sufferings of Mrs. Jemima Howe
(Vernon, Vermont), 1755,
with letters relating to her captivity
88

The Captivity of Zadock Steele
(Royalton, Vermont), 1780
100

George Avery's Journal of the Royalton Raid
(Royalton, Vermont), 1780
150

Suggestions for Further Reading
159

Introduction

Pioneers on the American frontier commonly viewed the prospect of being taken captive by Indians as a fate worse than death. The narratives recorded by redeemed captives represent one of the oldest genres of American literature, and they helped to establish enduring stereotypes of Indians as cruel and bloodthirsty. More recently, scholars have looked again at captivity narratives as sources of information on Indian societies and cultural interaction on the American frontier. The narratives reprinted in this volume come from Vermont and New Hampshire, focused in the Connecticut Valley watershed between the Green and White mountains, and mainly from the second half of the eighteenth century. They provide insights into life and experiences on the north country frontier and into the nature of relations between the colonists and the local Abenaki Indians. They are also fascinating stories of individual endurance and resilience, and of ordinary people caught up in international and interethnic conflicts.

Many of the earliest accounts of Indian captivities came from southern and central New England during almost a century of warfare between settlers and Indians, and showed the heavy influence of Puritan pens. The Puritans interpreted conflict with the Indians as a Holy War waged in the wilderness against the forces of Satan. Indian raids were seen as a form of divine punishment visited upon erring communities and an Indian captivity was a testing of Christian resolve in the hands of the Devil's agents. A theme of bondage and redemption pervaded Puritan captivity narratives: the hero or heroine was abducted from home, dragged through the wilderness, taken into Indian society, but eventually liberated and returned home. Survival of the ordeal was a sign of God's infinite power and mercy. Puritan ministers used the captives' stories in their sermons and biblical allusions laced the captivity narratives published in Puritan New England. In these early captivity narratives, the Indians, like their forest home, served as symbols and rarely emerged from the pages as human beings.

By the second half of the eighteenth century, however, Puritan influence had declined considerably and captivity narratives, though often still couched in religious terms and carrying a moral lesson, became less dominated by religious symbolism and metaphorical structures. More-over, in northern frontier regions, where population pressure was less intense, settlers frequently experienced closer contact with Indian neighbors—neighbors who in different circumstances sometimes became captors. The French and Indian war party that conducted the famous raid on Deerfield, Massachusetts, in 1704 was large and carried off over one hundred captives. By contrast, Indian raids in the north country of Vermont and New Hampshire generally consisted of small parties of Abenakis and usually netted a handful of captives. As a result, captives and captors were more likely to come to know each other during the long trek north, and captives, considered a scarce commodity, may have received better treatment. The north country narratives reprinted in this volume may be less famous than those of Mary Rowlandson and John Williams in Massachusetts but they more often portray Indian captors as human individuals rather than agents of the Devil, and they also offer glimpses of the daily life of frontier communities that existed on the edges of Indian country.

Whereas Puritan writers portrayed Indian raiders as faceless savages intent on butchery, the reality of Indian-white interaction, even in captivity, was far more complex. Indian war parties from the north traveled south along familiar trails, often struck places they had once inhabited, and sometimes knew the people they took captive. The north country frontier was not a racial battle line; it was a porous zone of interaction where colonists and Indians lived alongside each other as often as they fought, where cautious coexistence was more usual than open conflict.

Puritan chroniclers and early New England historians depicted the triumph of English settlers over what they saw as a savage wilderness. They made little effort to understand Indian captors or their reasons for taking captives. They attributed Indian raids to the natural ferocity of the Indians or the intrigues of unscrupulous French Catholics in Canada and depicted Indian warriors as shadowy figures who slipped from the forest to commit mayhem and carry women and children into unspeakable bondage. The possibility that warriors might offer humane treatment to their prisoners was barely considered. The narratives of Indian captives themselves, however, often offer a clearer picture of the nature and purpose of captive-taking, challenge old stereotypes about Indian brutality, and hint at a wider dimension of interethnic contact on the north country frontier.

Indians often launched raids for the specific purpose of taking captives, and war parties sometimes took along thongs and extra moccasins for the prisoners they expected to take. Taking captives was a long-established practice in Indian warfare, with adopted captives filling the place of deceased relatives and, as warfare escalated in the woodlands of northeastern America, it became a vital means of maintaining population levels. With the waging of the imperial wars between France and England from 1689 to 1763, captive-taking became a means of weakening the English enemy to the south and also a source of revenue as French allies now bought the Indians' prisoners for ransom to the English. Over sixteen hundred people were taken captive from New England during the French and Indian wars; some died in captivity; many were sold to the French and either ransomed to the English or made new lives for themselves in French Canada; some were adopted into Indian communities.

The Champlain, Connecticut, and Merrimack valleys provided avenues for Indian raiding parties and for their captives. Hundreds of captives abducted from throughout New England followed trails through New Hampshire and Vermont to Indian villages in the north and French towns in Canada. The route that ran from Lake Champlain, up the Winooski River, across the Green Mountains, and down the Black River to the Connecticut and south to the English settlements was traveled so frequently by Indian war parties—and in reverse with their captives—that it became known simply as "the Indian road"; and it was only one of many such routes through the region.

Indian war parties struck suddenly and many captives fell into their hands in shock and bewilderment. The captives' subsequent fortunes often depended on the individual warrior who seized them. Anxious to round up their prisoners and head north before pursuit could be mounted from neighboring settlements, the Indians pushed their captives hard in the initial stages of the journey. Warriors far from home and running for their lives sometimes tomahawked captives too weak to keep up. As the Indians' apprehension of being overtaken diminished, so did the likelihood that captives would be executed.

For most captives, the march into captivity produced the greatest physical hardship. Raids sometimes took place in dead of winter and the return journey north—which could take as long as three months—was an arduous trek for people dragged from their homes without adequate food or clothing. Exhaustion, cold, and frostbite took their toll. Susanna Johnson compared the march into captivity to a funeral procession.

Many of the sufferings that captives endured were a product of Indian life-style rather than deliberate cruelty. Accustomed to recurrent periods of feast and famine, inured to life in country that whites regarded as a wilderness, and living a life of regular mobility, Indians made few special provisions for their captives—Susanna Johnson's experience in child-birth being a notable exception. What whites regarded as a cruel pace, an unsavory diet, and flimsy shelter were often the norm for their captors. Starvation faced many raiding parties and though Indians usually shared what they had with their captives, Indian generosity could not compensate for European distaste for native food, and occasional Indian kindnesses provided little comfort in the midst of the ordeal.

Nevertheless, captives regularly noted instances of humane treatment by their captors. The prisoners' market value in French Canada and the possibility of their adoption into Indian families helped shield them from abuse. Many confessed they had never expected such kind treatment from supposed "savages." Puritan propaganda portrayed Indians dashing out infants' brains and ravishing defenseless females, but warriors often carried captive children all the way to Canada and invariably treated women with civility, as illustrated by the experiences of Isabella McCoy and Susanna Johnson. Indians abstained from sex on the warpath and a warrior would not force himself on a woman who might be adopted as his sister after they were back at the village. Even so, outbursts of occasional violence, instances of individual caprice, psychological threats, and the transforming influence of alcohol, which Nehemiah How witnessed upon his captors when they called at Crown Point on Lake Champlain—all kept captives in constant fear and made the journey north a nightmare.

The grueling trek north was only the beginning of the captivity experience. Arrival at Indian villages ushered in a new life for the captives, if only temporarily. Some prisoners were sold immediately to the French but many others were adopted into Indian families. Indian warriors who showed considerate treatment, shared native food and clothing, and demanded rapid adjustment to Indian ways, may have been preparing the way for adoption and acceptance. Rituals of adoption involved washing the captives and dressing them in Indian clothing, as George Avery found, but the dreaded ordeal of running the gauntlet as experienced by the Johnson family proved to be largely a symbolic event. After adoptees had undergone the required initiation rites, they were accepted as members of the family and could expect to be treated with the respect and generosity that cemented relations in Abenaki communities.

Jemima Howe's account suggests that the greatest hardship for female captives was the mental and emotional strain of being carried far from home and family, and in some cases the agony of being separated from one's children. The Abenakis who attacked Bridgman's Fort in 1755 marched Mrs. Howe and most of her children to St. Francis, but her ten-year-old daughter, Submit, was sold to Governor Pierre de Vaudreuil and placed in a convent. Mary, her thirteen-year-old daughter, was to marry an Indian, but Vaudreuil intervened and had her sent to the same convent. Jemima's youngest child died in captivity. After her own liberation, Mrs. Howe was able to secure Submit's release from the convent despite the girl's desire to remain. Mary, however, married a Frenchman and refused to rejoin her family.

A number of people found their new way of life preferable to their old and became "white Indians." Children adjusted most easily to Indian life, as Susanna Johnson found when she was reunited with her eleven-year-old son Sylvanus after a four-year separation, but adults were not immune to the pull of Indian society. Mary Fowler and Susanna Johnson both found life hard in Indian villages, but such captives as Isabella McCoy returned home reluctantly, knowing women could expect little better in frontier white communities. Some captives chose to remain with their adopted Indian families even when given the chance to return home. As Phineas Stevens's accounts of his missions to Canada indicate, Abenakis were reluctant to release captives they had adopted, and captives who had been adopted often had no desire to return home. A former captive himself, Stevens knew that the bonds between an adopted captive and an Indian family often remained strong even after redemption.

Captives and their offspring brought a substantial influx of European culture into Indian communities. Joseph Louis Gill, the Abenaki chief who adopted Susanna Johnson at St. Francis, was the son of English parents who had been abducted as children, baptized as Roman Catholics, raised as Abenakis, and lived the rest of their lives with the Indians. Eleazar Wheelock regularly sought sons of "white Indians" for his "Indian school," and most of the Canadian Indian students enrolled at Dartmouth College at the time of the American Revolution were descendants of English captives.

Individuals who were liberated from the Indians often found that readjustment to life in colonial society could be traumatic. Others never forgot what they had learned while they lived with the Indians. As white captives added a new element to the cultural fabric of Indian societies, so "white Indians" who returned home added another dimension to colonial society on the northern frontier and played an important role as intermediaries between the settlers and the Indians. Phineas Stevens was captured by the Abenakis when he was sixteen. He learned to speak Abenaki and after his redemption he traded with and trusted them, as well as fighting against them and their French allies. He became a pivotal figure on the upper Connecticut in the middle of the eighteenth century and undertook several missions to attempt to redeem New England captives in Canada. Sylvanus Johnson, another captive taken as a boy and later redeemed, apparently often expressed regret at being ransomed. He lived out his later years in Walpole, New Hampshire, dying at 84 in 1832 with the reputation of an "honest and upright man," but he steadfastly maintained that the Indians with whom he spent his boyhood were morally superior to the whites among whom he lived his adult life.

While some captives disappeared without trace into Indian villages, many others went from Indian into French or British hands. Such a transfer could lead to a new life or be the first step toward returning home via ransom or an exchange of prisoners. When white communities were at war with each other, however, passage into non-Indian hands was a mixed blessing and generated ambivalent responses from captives. As Nehemiah How and Zadock Steele found, eighteenth-century prisoners of war sometimes experienced harsher treatment from European jailors than from Indian captors. New Hampshire's General John Stark, who was captured by Abenakis in 1752 and redeemed by Phineas Stevens, said he "experienced more genuine kindness from the savages of St. Francis, than he ever knew prisoners of war to receive from any civilized nation."

Captives who never returned home usually produced no books. Those captives who recounted their stories for publication had chosen not to live as Indians and therefore provided a revealing but rather one-sided view of Indian life. Whatever kindnesses Indians showed them, captives experienced a harrowing ordeal and their accounts, whether from their own mouths or the pens of those who took down their stories, tended to dwell on human suffering, to spell out moral lessons, and to belabor God's role as the arbiter of human destinies. Such narratives remained popular long after Indian captivity ceased to be a peril for frontier settlers. They served different purposes for different generations, and they remain open to a variety of interpretations. Yet beneath their often lop-sided content and dated style, captivity narratives open a window into the lives of people, Indian and white, who inhabited Vermont and New Hampshire over two hundred years ago. The captives' accounts reprinted in this volume—and the account of George Avery published here for the first time—show that Indians and colonists influenced each other's lives in ways that were both dramatic and subtle. They might also prompt us to pause and consider how much the society that emerged in this part of the country owed, then as now, to layers of interaction between natives and newcomers.

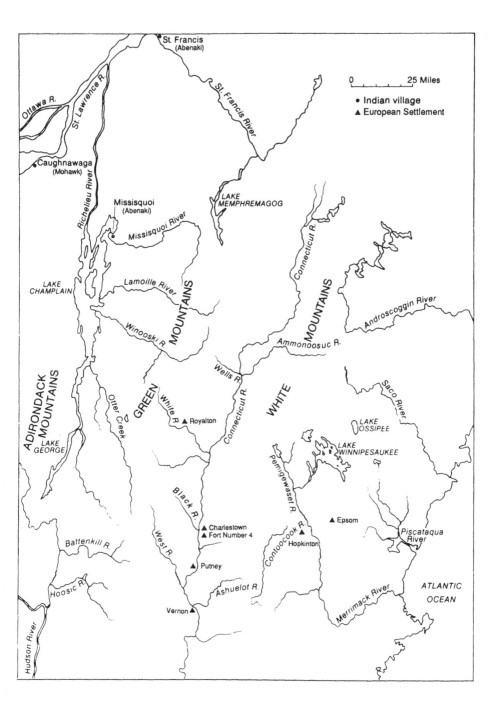

The North Country showing the villages of the captors and captives.

North Country Captives

NEHEMIAH HOW

Militia captain Nehemiah How was probably the first captive taken from the Connecticut Valley in King George's War (1744–48). Abenaki Indians from St. Francis surprised him while he was out cutting wood, marched him across the Green Mountains to Crown Point, then north to Canada. He was taken to Quebec and interrogated by the French for news of developments in New England and Europe. After a week in the guard house, How was sent to the prison, never to emerge. He led his fellow-prisoners in prayers and Bible readings, and recorded their deaths to prison fever in his journal. How's journal ended suddenly and a fellow prisoner recorded in his journal that on May 24, 1747 "Died Nehemiah how of ye Fever, A Good Pious Old Gentleman aged Near 60 Years has been In prison Near 18 months and ye most Contented and Easy of any man in my Prison."

How's wife was Margaret Willard, who bore twelve children. One son, Caleb, was the second husband of Jemima Howe, and was killed by Indians. A nephew, Daniel, was twice captured by Indians during King George's War, joining Nehemiah in the Quebec jail during the first captivity and securing final release at the end of the war.

[Emma Lewis Coleman, *New England Captives Carried to Canada, 1677–1760* 2 vols. (Portland, Maine: Southworth Press, 1925) 2: 178–80; "Relation du Capitaine How, fait prisonnier au Fort No. 2, Novembre 9, 1745," in *Collection De Manuscrits Contenant Lettres, Mémoires, et Autres Documents Historiques Rélatifs a La Nouvelle-France* 4 vols. (Quebec, 1883–85) 3: 268–70; Captain William Pote's Journal during his captivity among the French and Indians, May 1745–Aug. 1747, Newberry Library, Chicago, Ayer Manuscript No. 733.]

A Narrative

of the captivity of Nehemiah How, who was taken by the Indians at the Great Meadow fort above Fort Dummer, where he was an inhabitant, October 11TH, 1745. Giving an account of what he met with in his travelling to Canada, and while he was in prison there. Together with an account of Mr. How's death at Canada.—Psalm CXXXVII: 1, 2, 3, and 4.—Boston: N.E. Printed and sold opposite to the Prison in Queen Street, 1748.

AT THE Great Meadow's fort, fourteen miles above fort Dummer, October 11th, 1745, where I was an inhabitant, I went out from the fort about fifty rods to cut wood; and when I had done, I walked towards the fort, but in my way heard the crackling of fences behind me, and turning about, saw twelve or thirteen Indians, with red painted heads, running after me; on which I cried to God for help, and ran, and hallooed as I ran, to alarm the fort. But by the time I had run ten rods, the Indians came up with me and took hold of me. At the same time the men at the fort shot at the Indians, and killed one on the spot, wounded another, who died fourteen days after he got home, and likewise shot a bullet through the powder-horn of one that had hold of me. They then led me into the swamp and pinioned me. I then committed my case to God, and prayed that, since it was his will to deliver me into the hands of those cruel men, I might find favor in their eyes; which request God in his infinite mercy was pleased to grant; for they were generally kind to me while I was with them. Some of the Indians at that time took charge of me, others ran into the field to kill cattle. They led me about half a mile, where we staid in open sight of the fort, till the Indians who were killing cattle came to us, laden with beef. Then they went a little further to a house, where they staid to cut the meat from the bones, and cut the helve off of my axe, and stuck it into the ground, pointing the way we went.

Then we travelled along the river side, and when we had got about three miles, I espied a canoe coming down on the further side of the river, with David Rugg and Robert Baker, belonging to our fort. I made as much noise as I could, by hammering, &c., that they might see us before the Indians saw them, and so get ashore and escape. But the Indians saw them, and shot across the river, twenty or thirty guns at them, by which the first-mentioned man was killed, but the other, Robert Baker, got ashore and escaped. Then some of the Indians swam across the river and brought the canoe to us; having stripped and scalped the dead man, and then we went about a mile further, when we came to another house, where we stopped. While there we heard men running by the bank of the river, whom I knew to be Jonathan Thayer, Samuel Nutting and my son Caleb How. Five of the Indians ran to head them. My heart asked for them, and prayed to God to save them from the hands of the enemy. I suppose they hid under the bank of the river, for the Indians were gone some time, but came back without them, blessed be God.

We went about a mile further, where we lodged that night, and roasted the meat they had got. The next day we travelled very slow, by reason of the wounded Indian, which was a great favor to me. We lodged the second night against Number Four [since Charlestown, N.H.] The third day we likewise travelled slowly, and stopped often to rest, and get along the wounded man. We lodged that night by the second small river that runs into the great river against Number Four.

The fourth day morning the Indians held a piece of bark, and bid me write my name, and how many days we had travelled; "for," said they "may be Englishmen will come here." That was a hard day for me, as it was wet and we went over prodigious mountains, so that I became weak and faint; for I had not eaten the value of one meal from the time I was taken, and that being beef almost raw without bread or salt. When I came first to the foot of those hills, I thought it was impossible for me to ascend them, without immediate help from God; therefore my constant recourse was to him for strength, which he was graciously pleased to grant me, and for which I desire to praise him.

We got that day a little before night to a place where they had a hunting house, a kettle, some beer, Indian corn, and salt. They boiled a good mess of it. I drank of the broth, eat of the meat and corn, and was wonderfully refreshed, so that I felt like another man. The next morning we got up early, and after we had eaten, my master said to me, "You must quick walk to day, or I kill you." I told him I would go as fast as I could, and no faster, if he did kill me. At which an old Indian, who was the best friend I had, took care of me. We travelled that day very hard, and over steep hills, but it being a cool, windy day, I performed it with more ease than before; yet I was much tired before night, but dare not complain.

The next day the Indians gave me a pair of their shoes, so that I travelled with abundant more ease than when I wore my own shoes. I ate but very little, as our victuals were almost spent. When the sun was about two hours high, the Indians scattered to hunt, and they soon killed a fawn, and three small bears, so that we had again meat enough; some of which we boiled and eat heartily of, by which I felt strong.

The next day we travelled very hard, and performed it with ease, insomuch that one of the Indians told me I was a very strong man. About three o'clock we came to the lake, where they had five canoes, pork, Indian corn, and tobacco. We got into the canoes, and the Indians stuck up a pole about eight feet long with the scalp of David Rugg on the top of it painted red, with the likeness of eyes and mouth on it. We sailed about ten miles, and then went on shore, and after we had made a fire, we boiled a good supper, and eat heartily.

The next day we set sail for Crown Point, but when we were within a mile of the place, they went on shore, where were eight or ten French and Indians, two of whom, before I got on shore, came running into the water, knee deep, and pulled me out of the canoe. There they sung and danced around me a while, when one of them bid me sit down, which I did. Then they pulled off my shoes and buckles, and took them from me. Soon after we went along to Crown Point. When we got there, the

people, both French and Indians, were very thick by the water-side. Two
of the Indians took me out of the canoe, and leading me, bid me run,
which I did, about twenty rods to the fort. The fort is large, built with
stone and lime. They led me up to the third loft, where was the captain's
chamber. A chair was brought that I might sit by the fire and warm me.
Soon after, the Indians that I belonged to, and others that were there,
came into the chamber, among whom was one I knew, named *Pealtomy*.
He came and spoke to me, and shook hands with me, and brought to
me another Indian, named Amrusus, husband to her who was Eunice
Williams, daughter of the late Rev. John Williams, of Deerfield; he was
glad to see me, and I to see him. He asked me about his wife's relations,
and showed a great deal of respect to me.

A while after this, the Indians sat in a ring in the chamber, and Pealtomy came to me, and told me I must go and sing and dance before the
Indians. I told him I could not. He told me over some Indian words, and
bid me sing them. I told him I could not. With that the rest of the fort
who could speak some English, came to me, and bid me sing it in English, which was, "I don't know where I go," which I did, dancing round
that ring three times. I then sat down by the fire. The priest came to me,
and gave me a dram of rum, and afterwards the captain brought me part
of a loaf of bread and a plate of butter, and asked me to eat, which I did
heartily, for I had not eaten any bread from the time I was taken till then.
The French priest and all the officers showed me a great deal of respect.
The captain gave me a pair of good buck-skin shoes, and the priest fixed
them on my feet. We staid there that night, and I slept with the priest,
captain and lieutenant. The lieutenant's name was Ballock; he had been
a prisoner at Boston, and had been at Northampton and the towns thereabouts. This day, which was the Sabbath, I was well treated by the
French officers, with victuals and drink. We tarried there till noon, then
went off about a mile, and put on shore, where they staid the most of
the day; and having rum with them, most of them were much liquored.
Pealtomy and his squaw, and another Indian family, went with us, and
by them I found out that William Phips killed an Indian, besides him
we wounded before he was killed; for an Indian who was with us asked
me if there was one killed near our fort last summer. I told him I did
not know. He said he had a brother who went out then, and he had not
seen him since, and had heard he was killed at our fort, and wanted to
know if it was true. But I did not think it best to tell him any such thing
was suspected.

The Indians now got into a frolic, and quarrelled about me, and made
me sit in the canoe by the water-side. I was afraid they would hurt if

not kill me. They attempted to come to me, but the sober Indians hindered them that were in liquor. Pealtomy seeing the rout, went to the fort, and soon after, Lieut. Ballock, with some soldiers, came to us, and when the Indians were made easy, they went away. We lodged there that night, and the next day was a stormy day of wind, snow and rain, so that we were forced to tarry there that day and the next night. In this time the Indians continued fetching rum from the fort, and kept half drunk. Here I underwent some hardship by staying there so long in a storm without shelter or blanket. They had a great dance that night, and hung up David Rugg's scalp on a pole, dancing round it. After they had done, they lay down to sleep.

The next morning, which was the tenth day from the time of my being taken, we went off in the canoe, and the night after we arrived at the wide lake, and there we staid that night. Some of the Indians went a hunting, and killed a fat deer, so that we had victuals plenty, for we had a full supply of bread given us at the fort at Crown Point.

The next morning the wind being calm, we set about two hours before day, and soon after came to a schooner lying at anchor. We went on board her, and the French treated us very civilly. They gave each of us a dram of rum, and victuals to eat. As soon as it was day we left the schooner, and two hours before sunset got over the lake, and next day came to Shamballee [Chamblee,] where we met three hundred French and two hundred Indians, who did the mischief about Mr. Lydius' fort. I was taken out of the canoe by two Frenchmen, and fled to a house about ten rods off as fast as I could run, the Indians flinging snow-balls at me. As soon as I got to the house, the Indians stood round me very thick, and bid me sing and dance, which I did with them, in their way; then they gave a shout, and left off. Two of them came to me, one of whom smote me on one cheek, the other on the other, which made the blood run plentifully. Then they bid me sing and dance again, which I did with them, and they with me, shouting as before. Then two Frenchmen took me under each arm, and ran so fast that the Indians could not keep up with us to hurt me. We ran about forty rods to another house, where a chair was brought for me to sit down. The house was soon full of French and Indians, and others surrounded it, and some were looking in to the windows. A French gentleman came to me, took me by the hand, and led me into a small room, where none came in but such as he admitted. He gave me victuals and drink. Several French gentlemen and Indians came in and were civil to me. The Indians who came in could speak English, shook hands with me, and called me brother. They told me they were all soldiers, and were going to New England. They said they should go to my town, which was a great damp to my spirits, till I heard of their return, where they had been, and what they had done. A while after this, the Indians whom I belonged to came to me and told me we must go. I went with them. After going down the river about two miles, we came to the thickest of the town, where was a large fort built with stone and lime, and very large and fine houses in it. Here was the general of the army I spoke of before. He asked me what news from London and Boston. I told him such stories as I thought convenient, and omitted the rest, and then went down to the canoes. Some of the Indians went and got a plenty of bread and beef, which they put into the canoes, and then we went into a French house, where we had a good supper. There came in several French gentlemen to see me, who were civil. One of them gave me a crown, sterling. We lodged there till about two hours before day, when we arose, and went down the river. I suppose we went a hundred miles that day, which brought us into a great river, called Quebec. We lodged that night in a French house, and were civilly treated.

The next day we went down the river, and I was carried before the governor there, which was the Sabbath, and the 16th day after my being taken. We staid there about three hours, and were well treated by the French. The Indians were then ordered to carry me down to Quebec, which was ninety miles further. We went down the river about three miles that night, then going on shore, lodged the remainder of the night.

The next morning we set off, and the second day, which was the 18th from the time I was taken, we arrived at Quebec. The land is inhabited on both sides of the river from the lake to Quebec, which is at least two hundred miles, especially below Chamblee, very thick, so that the houses are within sight of one another all the way.

But to return: After we arrived at Quebec, I was carried up into a large chamber, which was full of Indians, who were civil to me. Many of the French came in to see me, and were also very kind. I staid there about two hours, when a French gentleman, who could speak good English, came in and told me I must go with him to the governor, which I did; and after answering a great many questions, and being treated with as much bread and wine as I desired, I was sent with an officer to the guard-house, and led into a small room, where was an Englishman named William Stroud, a kinsman of the Hon. Judge Lynd, in New England. He belonged to South Carolina, and had been at Quebec six years. The governor kept him confined for fear he should leave him and go to New England, and discover their strength. Mr. Stroud and I were kept in the guard-house one week, with a sufficiency of food and drink.

The French gentlemen kept coming in to see me, and I was very civilly treated by them. I had the better opportunity of discoursing with them, as Mr. Stroud was a good interpreter.

After this we were sent to prison, where I found one James Kinlade, who was taken fourteen days before I was, at Sheepscot, at the eastward, in New England. I was much pleased with his conversation, esteeming him a man of true piety. We were kept in prison eight days, with liberty to keep in the room with the prison-keeper. We were daily visited by gentlemen and ladies, who showed us great kindness in giving us money and other things, and their behavior towards us was pleasant. Blessed be God therefor, for I desire to ascribe all the favors I have been the partaker of, ever since my captivity, to the abundant grace and goodness of a bountiful God, as the first cause.

After this Mr. Kinlade and I were sent to another prison, where were twenty-two seamen belonging to several parts of our king's dominions; three of them captains of vessels, viz. James Southerland of Cape Cod, William Chipman of Marblehead, William Pote of Casco Bay. This prison was a large house, built with stone and lime, two feet thick, and about one hundred and twenty feet long. We had two large stoves in it, and wood enough, so that we could keep ourselves warm in the coldest weather. We had provision sufficient, viz. two pounds of good wheat bread, one pound of beef, and peas answerable, to each man, ready dressed every day.

When I had been there a few days, the captives desired me to lead them in carrying on morning and evening devotion, which I was willing to do. We had a Bible, psalm-book, and some other good books. Our constant practice was to read a chapter in the Bible, and sing part of a psalm, and to pray, night and morning.

When I was at the first prison, I was stripped of all my old and lousy clothes, and had other clothing given me from head to foot, and had many kindnesses shown me by those that lived thereabouts; more especially by one Mr. Corby and his wife, who gave me money there, and brought me many good things at the other prison. But here I was taken ill, as was also most of the other prisoners, with a flux, which lasted near a month, so that I was grown very weak. After that I was healthy, through divine goodness. Blessed be God for it.

I was much concerned for my country, especially for the place I was taken from, by reason that I met an army going thither, as they told me. The 27th day of November we had news come to the prison that this army had returned to Chamblee, and had taken upwards of a hundred captives, which increased my concern; for I expected our fort, and others thereabouts, were destroyed. This news put me upon earnest prayer to God that he would give me grace to submit to his will; after which I was easy in my mind.

About a fortnight after, a Dutchman was brought to prison, who was one of the captives the said army had taken. He told me they had burnt Mr. Lydius' fort, and all the houses at that new township, killed Capt. Schuyler and five or six more, and had brought fifty whites and about sixty negroes to Montreal. I was sorry to hear of so much mischief done, but rejoiced they had not been upon our river, and the towns thereabouts, for which I gave thanks to God for his great goodness in preserving them, and particularly my family.

When Christmas came, the governor sent us twenty-four livres, and the lord-intendant came into the prison and gave us twenty-four more, which was about two guineas. He told us he hoped we should be sent home in a little time. He was a pleasant gentleman, and very kind to captives. Some time after, Mr. Shearly, a gentleman of quality, came to us, and gave to the three sea captains twenty-four livres, and to me twelve, and the next day sent me a bottle of claret wine. About ten days after he sent me twelve livres more; in all eight pounds, old tenor.

January 20th, 1746, eighteen captives were brought from Montreal to the prison at Quebec, which is 180 miles.

February 22d, seven captives more, who were taken at Albany, were brought to the prison to us, viz. six men and one old woman seventy years old, who had been so infirm for seven years past that she had not been able to walk the streets, yet performed this tedious journey with ease.

March 15th, one of the captives taken at Albany, after fourteen or fifteen days' sickness, died in the hospital at Quebec,—a man of a sober, pious conversation. His name was Lawrence Plaffer, a German born.

May 3d, three captives taken at No. Four, sixteen miles above where I was taken, viz. Capt. John Spafford, Isaac Parker, and Stephen Farnsworth, were brought to prison to us. They informed me my family was well, a few days before they were taken, which rejoiced me much. I was sorry for the misfortune of these my friends, but was glad of their company, and of their being well used by those who took them.

May 14th, two captives were brought into prison, Jacob Read and Edward Cloutman, taken at a new township called Gorhamtown, near Casco Bay. They informed us that one man and four children of one of them were killed, and his wife taken at the same time with them, and was in the hands of the Indians.

May 16th, two lads, James and Samuel Anderson, brothers, taken at Sheepscot, were brought to prison. On the 17th, Samuel Burbank and David Woodwell, who were taken at New Hopkinton, near Rumford, [Concord, N.H.] were brought to prison, and informed us there were taken with them two sons of the said Burbank, and the wife, two sons and a daughter of the said Woodwell, whom they left in the hands of the Indians.

May 24th, Thomas Jones, of Holliston, who was a soldier at Con-toocook, was brought to prison, and told us that one Elisha Cook, and a negro belonging to the Rev. Mr. Stevens, were killed when he was taken.

June 1st, William Aikings, taken at Pleasant Point, near fort George, was brought to prison. June 2d, Mr. Shearly brought several letters of deacon Timothy Brown, of Lower Ashuelot, and money, and delivered them to me, which made me think he was killed or taken. A few days after, Mr. Shearly told me he was taken. I was glad to hear he was alive.

June 6th, Timothy Cummings, aged 60, was brought to prison, who informed us he was at work with five other men, about forty rods from the block-house, George's [fort,] when five Indians shot at them, but hurt none. The men ran away, and left him and their guns to the Indians. He told us that the ensign was killed as he stood on the top of the fort, and that the English killed five Indians at the same time.

June 13th, Mr. Shearly brought to the captives some letters which were sent from Albany, and among them one from Lieut. Gov. Phips, of the Massachusetts Bay, to the governor of Canada, for the exchange of prisoners, which gave us great hopes of a speedy release.

June 22d, eight men were brought to prison, among whom were dea-con Brown and Robert Morse, who informed me that there were six or eight Indians killed, a little before they were taken, at Upper Ashuelot, and that they learnt, by the Indians who took them, there were six more of the English killed at other places near Connecticut river, and several more much wounded; these last were supposed to be the wife and chil-dren of the aforesaid Burbank and Woodwell.

July 5th, we sent a petition to the chief governor that we might be exchanged, and the 7th, Mr. Shearly told us we should be exchanged for other captives in a little time, which caused great joy among us. The same day, at night, John Berran, of Northfield, was brought to prison, who told us that an expedition against Canada was on foot, which much rejoiced us. He also told us of the three fights in No. Four, and who were killed and taken, and of the mischief done in other places near Connecticut river, and that my brother Daniel How's son Daniel was taken with him, and was in the hands of the Indians, who designed to keep him.

July 20th, John Jones, a seaman, was brought into prison, who told us he was going from Cape Breton to Newfoundland with one Englishman and four Frenchmen, who had sworn allegiance to King George, and in the passage they killed the other Englishman, but carried him to the bay of Arb, where there was an army of French and Indians, to whom they delivered him, and by them was sent to Quebec.

July 21st, John Richards and a boy of nine or ten years of age, who belonged to Rochester, in New Hampshire, were brought to prison. They told us there were four Englishmen killed when they were taken.

August 15th, seven captives, who with eight more taken at St. John's Island, were brought to prison. They told us that several were killed after quarters were given, among whom was James Owen, late of Brookfield, in New England. On the 16th, Thomas Jones, late of Sherburne, in New England, after seven or eight days' sickness, died. He gave good satisfaction as to his future state. On the 25th we had a squall of snow.

September 12th, Robert Downing, who had been a soldier at Cape Breton, and was taken at St. Johns, and who was with the Indians two months, and suffered great abuse from them, was brought to prison.

On the 15th, twenty-three of the captives taken at Hoosuck fort were brought to prison, among whom was the Rev. Mr. John Norton. They informed us that after fighting twenty-five hours, with eight hundred French and Indians, they surrendered themselves, on capitulation, prisoners of war; that Thomas Nalton and Josiah Read were killed when they were taken. The names of those now brought in are the Rev. Mr. Norton, John Hawks, John Smead, his wife and six children, John Perry and his wife, Moses Scott, his wife and two children, Samuel Goodman, Jonathan Bridgman, Nathan Eames, Joseph Scott, Amos Pratt, Benjamin Sinconds, Samuel Lovet, David Warren, and Phinehas Furbush. The two last of these informed me that my brother Daniel How's son was taken from the Indians, and now lives with a French gentleman at Montreal. There were four captives more taken at Albany, the last summer, who were brought to prison the same day.

On the 26th (Sept.) 74 men and two women, taken at sea, were brought to prison. October 1st, Jacob Shepard, of Westborough, taken at Hoosuck, was brought to prison. On the 3d, Jonathan Batherick was brought in, and on the 5th, seventeen other men, three of whom were taken with Mr. Norton and others, viz. Nathaniel Hitchcock, John Aldrick, and Stephen Scott. Richard Subs, who was taken at New Casco, says one man was killed at the same time. Also Pike Gooden, taken at Saco, was brought to prison. He says he had a brother killed at the same time. On the 12th, twenty-four seamen are brought in, and on the 19th, six more. On the 20th, Jacob Read died. On the 23d, Edward Cloutman and Robert Dunbar broke prison and escaped for New England. The 27th, a man was brought into prison, who said the Indians took five more [besides himself], and brought ten scalps to Montreal.

November 1st, John Read died. The 9th, John Davis, taken with Mr. Norman, died. The 17th, Nathan Eames, of Marlborough, died. On the 19th, Mr. Adams, taken at Sheepscot, is brought to prison. He says that James Anderson's father was killed, and his uncle taken at the same time. The 20th, Leonard Lydle and the widow Sarah Briant were married in Canada, by the Rev. Mr. Norton. On the 22d, the abovesaid Anderson's uncle was brought to prison. Two days after, (24th) John Bradshaw died. He had not been well for most of the time he had been a prisoner. It is a very melancholy time with us. There are now thirty sick, and deaths among us daily. Died on the 28th, Jonathan Dunham, and on the 29th, died also Capt. Bailey of Amesbury.

December 1st, an Albany man died, and on the 6th, Pike Gooden, who, we have reason to believe, made a happy change. On the 7th, a girl of ten years died. The 11th, Moses Scott's wife died, and on the 15th, one of Captain Robertson's lieutenants. Daniel Woodwell's wife died on the 18th, a pious woman. John Perry's wife died the 23d. On the 26th, William Dayly, of New York, died.

January 3d, 1747, Jonathan Harthan died. On the 12th, Phinehas Andrews, of Cape Ann, died. He was one of the twenty captives, who, the same night, had been removed to another prison, hoping thereby to get rid of the infection. Jacob Bailey, brother to Capt. Bailey, died the 15th, and the 17th, Giat Braban, Captain Chapman's carpenter, died. On the 23d, Samuel Lovet, son of Major Lovet, of Mendon, in New England, died.

February 10th, William Garwass died, also the youngest child of Moses Scott. The 15th, my nephew, Daniel How, and six more were brought down from Montreal to Quebec, viz. John Sunderland, John Smith, Richard Smith, William Scott, Philip Scoffil, and Benjamin Tainter, son to Lieutenant Tainter of Westborough in New England. The 23d, Richard Bennet died, and the 25th, Michael Dugon.

March 18th, James Margra died, and on the 22d, Capt. John Fort and Samuel Goodman; the 28th, the wife of John Smead died, and left six children, the youngest of whom was born the second night after the mother was taken.

April 7th, Philip Scaffield, [Scofield?] and next day John Saneld, the next day Capt. James Jordan and one of his men, died. On the 12th, Amos Pratt, of Shrewsbury, and on the 14th, Timothy Cummings, the 17th, John Dill, of Hull in New England, the 18th, Samuel Venhon, of Plymouth, died. On the 26th, Capt. Jonathan Williamson was brought to prison. He was taken at the new town on Sheepscot river. The same day came in, also, three men who were taken at Albany, three weeks before, and tell us that thirteen were killed, Capt. Trent being one. They were all soldiers for the expedition to Canada. On the 27th, Joseph Denox, and the 28th, Samuel Evans, died. The same night the prison took fire, and was burnt, but the things therein were mostly saved. We were kept that night under a guard.

May 7th, Sarah Lydle, whose name was Briant when she was taken, and married while a captive, died, and the 13th, Mr. Smead's son Daniel died, and Christian Tether the 14th. The same day died also Hezekiah Huntington, a hopeful youth, of a liberal education. He was a son of Colonel Huntington of Connecticut, in New England. On the 15th, Joseph Grey, and on the 19th Samuel Burbank, died. At the same time died two children who were put out to the French to nurse.

At this time I received a letter from Major Willard, dated March 17th, 1747, wherein he informs me my family were well, which was joyful news to me. May 19th, Abraham Fort died.

[from Samuel G. Drake, ed. *Indian Captivities, or Life in the Wigwam* (Auburn: Derby and Miller, 1852), 127–38.]

MARY FOWLER

—◦→⟫≫•◦≪⟪←◦—

Mary Fowler's family was captured by Abenakis during King George's War and taken to Canada. Mary was held captive at St. Francis, but her family was imprisoned in Quebec, where her mother died of yellow fever in December 1746. A fellow-prisoner, William Pote, described her in his journal as "a woman yt Bore an Exceedingly Good Charector among all ye Prisoners and Left behind her in this place, her husband and two Children and a Daughter in ye hands of ye Indians, aged about 18 Years." On one occasion, the prison inmates saw Mary when she was in the city with her adopted Indian family: "ye Girl was Dressed after ye manner of ye Indians with a Great quantity of wampan which ye Indians Call Extraordinary Embellishment." After the prisoners were released from Quebec at the end of the war, Mary's father made repeated efforts to secure her release and finally succeeded with the assistance of a French agent. When Mary was in her nineties she told the story of her captivity as it was printed in Samuel Drake's Indian Captivities. *She died in 1829, at about 100 years old.*

[Coleman, *New England Captives Carried to Canada* 2: 187–89; Journal of Captain William Pote, Newberry Library.]

Captivity of Mary Fowler, of Hopkinton

MARY FOWLER, formerly Mary Woodwell, now living in Canterbury in this state, was born in the town of Hopkinton, in Massachusetts, May 11, 1730. Her parents moved to Hopkinton in this state when she was about twelve years of age, and settled on the westerly side of what is called Putney's Hill.

On the 22d day of April, in the year 1746, while in the garrison at her father's house, six Indians, armed with muskets, tomahawks, knives, &c. broke into the garrison and took eight persons while in their beds, viz. the said Mary, her parents, two of her brothers, Benjamin and Thomas, Samuel Burbank, an aged man, and his two sons, Caleb and Jonathan. They carried them through the wilderness to St. Francis in Canada. Here Mary and Jonathan Burbank were detained for the term of three years, (though not in one family,) and the other six were carried prisoners to Quebec, where Burbank, the aged, and Mary's mother died of the yellow fever in prison. The other four were afterwards exchanged.

The circumstances relative to their being taken were as follows: Ten persons, viz. the eight above mentioned, Samuel Burbank's wife and a soldier, were secluded in the garrison for fear of being attacked by the Indians, who had been frequently scouting through Hopkinton and the other adjacent towns. Early on the morning of their captivity, Samuel Burbank left the garrison and went to the barn in order to feed the cattle before the rest were up, leaving the door unfastened. The Indians, who lay near in ambush, immediately sallied forth and took him. From this affrighted captive they got information that the garrison was weak, whereupon they rushed in, and took them all, except the soldier who escaped, and Burbank's wife, who secreted herself in the cellar. During this attack Mary's mother, being closely embraced by a sturdy Indian, wrested from his side a long knife, with which she was in the act of running him through, when her husband prevailed with her to desist, fearing the fatal consequences. However, she secured the deadly weapon, and before they commenced their march threw it into the well, from whence it was taken after the captives returned. Another Indian presented a musket to Mary's breast, intending to blow her through, when a chief by the name of Pennos, who had previously received numerous kindnesses from her father's family, instantly interfered, and kept him from his cruel design, taking her for his own captive.

After having arrived at St. Francis, Pennos sold Mary to a squaw of another family, while J. Burbank continued in some remote part of the neighborhood under his own master. Mary's father and brothers, after they were exchanged, solicited a contribution for her redemption, which was at last obtained with great difficulty for one hundred livres, through the stratagem of a French doctor; all previous efforts made by her father and brothers having failed. This tender parent, though reduced to poverty by the savages, and having no pecuniary assistance except what he received through the hand of charity from his distant friends, had frequently visited St. Francis in order to have an interview with his only daughter, and to compromise with her mistress, offering her a large sum for Mary's redemption, but all to no effect. She refused to let her go short of her weight in silver. Moreover, Mary had previously been told by her mistress that if she intimated a word to her father that she wanted to go home with him, she should never see his face again; therefore, when interrogated by him on this subject, she remained silent, through fear of worse treatment; yet she could not conceal her grief, for her internal agitation and distress of mind caused the tears to flow profusely from her eyes. Her father, at length, worn out with grief and toil, retired to Montreal, where he contracted with a Frenchman as an agent to effect, if possible, the purchase of his daughter. This agent, after having attempted a compromise several times in vain, employed a French physician, who was in high reputation among the Indians, to assist him. The doctor, under a cloak of friendship, secretly advised Mary to feign herself sick, as the only alternative, and gave her medicine for the purpose. This doctor was soon called upon for medical aid; and although he appeared to exert the utmost of his skill, yet his patient continued to grow worse. After making several visits to no effect, he at length gave her over as being past recovery, advising her mistress, as a real friend, to sell her the first opportunity for what she could get, even if it were but a small sum; otherwise, said he, she will die on your hands, and you must lose her. The squaw, alarmed at the doctor's ceremony, and the dangerous appearance of her captive, immediately contracted with the French agent for one hundred livres; whereupon Mary soon began to amend; and was shortly after conveyed to Montreal, where she continued six months longer among the French waiting for a passport.

Thus after having been compelled to three years' hard labor in planting and hoeing corn, chopping and carrying wood, pounding *samp*, gathering cranberries and other wild fruit for the market, &c., this young woman was at length redeemed from the merciless hands and cruel servitude of the savages, who had not only wrested her from her home, but also from the tender embraces of her parents, and from all social intercourse with her friends.

Jonathan Burbank was redeemed about the same time—became an officer, and was afterwards killed by the Indians in the French war. These sons of the forest supposing him to have been Rogers, their avowed enemy, rushed upon him and slew him without ceremony, after he had given himself up as a prisoner of war.

After six months' detention among the French at Montreal, Mary was conveyed (mostly by water) to Albany by the Dutch, who had proceeded to Canada in order to redeem their black slaves, whom the Indians had previously taken and carried thither; from thence she was conducted to the place of her nativity, where she continued about five years, and was married to one Jesse Corbett, by whom she had two sons. From thence they moved to Hopkinton in this state, to the place where Mary had been taken by the Indians. Corbett, her husband, was drowned in Almsbury river, (now Warner river,) in Hopkinton, in the year 1759, in attempting to swim across the river—was carried down into the Contoocook, thence into the Merrimack, and was finally taken up in Dunstable with his clothes tied fast to his head. Mary was afterwards married to a Jeremiah Fowler, by whom she had five children. She is now living in Canterbury, in the enjoyment of good health and remarkable powers of mind, being in the ninety-third year of her age. The foregoing narrative was written a few weeks since as she related it.

[from Samuel G. Drake, ed. *Indian Captivities, or Life in the Wigwam* (Auburn: Derby and Miller, 1852), 140–43.]

ISABELLA McCOY

---◦──≫─≫─••◄─◄◄◄◦──---

Charles McCoy was an early settler of Epsom from Londonderry, who "extended his farm by spotting trees around upon the mountain." After a captivity among the Indians and the French, Mrs. McCoy was liberated at the end of King George's War, though she did not return home with much enthusiasm. Her Abenaki captors were quite well known in the settlements on the New Hampshire frontier, and Plausawa and Sabatis were killed there on the eve of the Seven Years' War.

[Coleman, *New England Captives Carried to Canada* 2: 197; Nathaniel Bouton, ed., *New Hampshire Provincial Papers* 7 vols. (Concord, Nashua, and Manchester, 1867–73) 6: 262–66.]

The Captivity of Mrs. Isabella M'Coy, of Epsom, N.H.

Communicated by the Rev. Jonathan Curtis, of Epsom, to the New Hampshire Historical Collections, 1747

THE INDIANS were first attracted to the new settlements in the town of Epsom, N.H., by discovering M'Coy at Suncook, now Pembroke. This, as nearly as can be ascertained, was in the year 1747. Reports were spread of the depredations of the Indians in various places, and M'Coy had heard that they had been seen lurking about the woods at Penacook, now Concord. He went as far as Pembroke, ascertained that they were in the vicinity, was somewhere discovered by them, and followed home. They told his wife, whom they afterwards made prisoner, that they looked through cracks around the house, and saw what they had for supper that night. They, however, did not discover themselves till the second day after. They probably wished to take a little time to learn the strength and preparation of the inhabitants. The next day, Mrs. M'Coy, attended by their two dogs, went down to see if any of the other families had returned from the garrison. She found no one. On her return, as she was passing the block house, which stood near the present site of the meeting house, the dogs, which had passed round it, came running back growling and very much excited. Their appearance induced her to make the best of her way home. The Indians afterwards told her that they then lay concealed there, and saw the dogs when they came round.

M'Coy, being now strongly suspicious that the Indians were actually in the town, determined to set off the next day with his family for the garrison at Nottingham. His family now consisted of himself, his wife, and son John. The younger children were still at the garrison. They accordingly secured their house as well as they could, and all set off next morning, M'Coy and his son with their guns, though without ammunition, having fired away what they brought with them in hunting.

As they were travelling a little distance east of the place where the meeting house now stands, Mrs. M'Coy fell a little in the rear of the others. This circumstance gave the Indians a favorable opportunity for separating her from her husband and son. The Indians, three men and a boy, lay in ambush near the foot of Marden's hill, not far from the junction of the mountain road with the main road. Here they suffered M'Coy and his son to pass; but as his wife was passing them, they reached from the bushes, and took hold of her, charging her to make no noise, and covering her mouth with their hands, as she cried to her husband for assistance. Her husband, hearing her cries, turned, and was about coming to her relief; but he no sooner began to advance, than the Indians, expecting probably that he would fire upon them, began to raise their pieces, which she pushed one side, and motioned to her friends to make their escape, knowing that their guns were not loaded, and that they would doubtless be killed if they approached. They accordingly ran into the woods, and made their escape to the garrison. This took place August 21, 1747.

The Indians then collected together what booty they could obtain, which consisted of an iron trammel from Mr. George Wallace's, the apples of the only tree which bore in town, which was in the orchard now owned by Mr. David Griffin, and some other trifling articles, and prepared to set off with their prisoner for Canada.

Before they took their departure, they conveyed Mrs. M'Coy to a place near the little Suncook River, where they left her in the care of the young Indian, while the three men, whose names were afterwards ascertained to be Plausawa, Sabatis, and Christi, went away, and were for some time absent. During their absence, Mrs. M'Coy thought of attempting to make her escape. She saw opportunities when she thought she might despatch the young Indian with the trammel which, with other things, was left with them, and thus perhaps avoid some strange and barbarous death, or a long and distressing captivity. But, on the other hand, she knew not at what distance the others were. If she attempted to kill her young keeper, she might fail. If she effected her purpose in this, she might be pursued and overtaken by a cruel and revengeful foe, and then some dreadful death would be her certain portion. On the whole, she thought best to endeavor to prepare her mind to bear what might be no more than a period of savage captivity. Soon, however, the Indians returned, and put an end for the present to all thoughts of escape. From the direction in which they went and returned, and from their smutty appearance, she suspected what their business had been. She told them she guessed they had been burning her house. Plausawa, who could speak some broken English, informed her they had.

They now commenced their long and tedious journey to Canada, in which the poor captive might well expect that great and complicated sufferings would be her lot. She did indeed find the journey fatiguing, and her fare scanty and precarious. But in her treatment from the Indians she experienced a very agreeable disappointment. The kindness she received from them was far greater than she had expected from those who were so often distinguished for their cruelties. The apples they had gathered they saved for her, giving her one every day. In this way they lasted her as far on the way as Lake Champlain. They gave her the last as they were crossing that lake in their canoes. This circumstance gave to the tree on which the apples grew the name of "Isabel's tree," her name being Isabella. In many ways did they appear desirous of mitigating the distresses of their prisoner while on their tedious journey. When night came on, and they halted to repose themselves in the dark wilderness, Plausawa, the head man, would make a little couch in the leaves, a little way from theirs, cover her up with his own blanket, and there she was suffered to sleep undisturbed till morning. When they came to a river which must be forded, one of them would carry her over on his back. Nothing like insult or indecency did they ever offer her during the whole time she was with them. They carried her to Canada, and sold her as a servant to a French family, whence, at the close of that war, she returned home. But so comfortable was her condition there, and her husband being a man of rather a rough and violent temper, she declared she never should have thought of attempting the journey home, were it not for the sake of her children.

After the capture of Mrs. M'Coy, the Indians frequently visited the town, but never committed any very great depredations. The greatest damage they ever did to the property of the inhabitants was the spoiling of all the ox teams in town. At the time referred to, there were but four yoke of oxen in the place, viz., M'Coy's, Captain M'Clary's, George

Wallace's, and Sergeant Blake's. It was a time of apprehension from the Indians, and the inhabitants had therefore all fled to the garrison at Nottingham. They left their oxen to graze about the woods, with a bell upon one of them. The Indians found them, shot one out of each yoke, took out their tongues, made a prize of the bell, and left them.

The ferocity and cruelty of the savages were doubtless very much averted by a friendly, conciliating course of conduct in the inhabitants towards them. This was particularly the case in the course pursued by Sergeant Blake. Being himself a curious marksman and an expert hunter,—traits of character in their view of the highest order,—he soon secured their respect, and, by a course of kind treatment, he secured their friendship to such a degree that, though they had opportunities, they would not injure him, even in time of war.

The first he ever saw of them was a company of them making towards his house through the opening from the top of Sanborn's Hill. He fled to the woods, and there lay concealed, till they had made a thorough search about his house and enclosures, and had gone off. The next time his visitors came, he was constrained to become more acquainted with them, and to treat them with more attention. As he was busily engaged towards the close of the day in completing a yard for his cow, the declining sun suddenly threw along several enormous shadows on the ground before him. He had no sooner turned to see the cause, than he found himself in the company of a number of stately Indians. Seeing his perturbation, they patted him on the head, and told him not to be afraid, for they would not hurt him. They then went with him into his house, and their first business was to search all his bottles, to see if he had any "*occapee*"—rum. They then told him they were very hungry, and wanted something to eat. He happened to have a quarter of a bear, which he gave them. They took it, and threw it whole upon the fire, and very soon began to cut and eat from it half raw. While they were eating, he employed himself in cutting pieces from it, and broiling upon a stick for them, which pleased them very much. After their repast, they wished for the privilege of lying by his fire through the night, which he granted. The next morning they proposed trying skill with him in firing at a mark. To this he acceded. But in this, finding themselves outdone, they were much astonished and chagrined; nevertheless, they highly commended him for his skill, patting him on the head, and telling him *if he would go off with them, they would make him their big captain.* They used often to call upon him, and his kindness to them they never forgot, even in time of war.

Plausawa had a peculiar manner of doubling his lip, and producing a very shrill, piercing whistle, which might be heard a great distance. At a time when considerable danger was apprehended from the Indians, Blake went off into the woods alone, though considered hazardous, to look for his cow that was missing. As he was passing along by Sinclair's Brook, an unfrequented place, northerly from M'Coy's Mountain, a very loud, sharp whistle, which he knew to be Plausawa's, suddenly passed through his head like the report of a pistol. The sudden alarm almost raised him from the ground, and, with a very light step, he soon reached home without his cow. In more peaceable times, Plausawa asked him if he did not remember the time, and laughed very much to think how he ran at the fright, and told him the reason for his whistling. *"Young Indian,"* said he, *"put up gun to shoot Englishman. Me knock it down, and whistle to start you off."* So lasting is their friendship, when treated well. At the close of the wars, the Indians built several wigwams near the confluence of Wallace's Brook with the great Suncook. On a little island in this river, near the place called "Short Falls," one of them lived for a considerable time. Plausawa and Sabatis were finally both killed in time of peace by one of the whites, after a drunken quarrel, and buried near a certain brook in Boscawen.

[from Francis Chase, ed., *Gathered Sketches from the Early History of New Hampshire and Vermont* (Claremont, N.H.: Tracy, Kenney & Co., 1856), 46–53.]

PHINEAS STEVENS

———◦≫≫≫•••≪≪≪◦———

Captain Phineas Stevens was one of the first settlers of Charlestown, or Fort Number Four, on the Connecticut River. He was a native of Sudbury, Massachusetts, from where his father, Deacon Stevens, moved to Rutland, Massachusetts. There, in August 1723, he and his youngest brother, Isaac, were captured by Grey Lock's Abenaki raiders: "By an Express arrived here from Rutland on Friday morning last, we are informed that on Wednesday last in the afternoon about 12 surpriz'd a Man and his four Sons as they were at Work in the Field at Rutland and took his Sons Prisoners but the Old Man made his Escape," said one report; other accounts said the Stevens family was surprised at the Rutland meeting house. The Abenakis killed two of the brothers and, according to local tradition, would have killed Isaac had not Phineas made them understand by signs that he would carry the child into captivity on his back.

Deacon Stevens raised money and made two trips to Canada to redeem his sons. Grey Lock gave Isaac to the Caughnawaga Indians near Montreal and the child apparently became so close to his adopted family that he was reluctant to return home. Phineas applied much of what he learned among the Abenakis in his later life as a trader, interpreter and soldier on the upper Connecticut River. He commanded successful defenses of Fort Number Four in 1746 and 1747, on the second occasion withstanding a two-day siege from the French and Indian army of Jean Baptiste Boucher de Niverville.

In 1749 the governor of Massachusetts appointed Stevens an emissary to Canada to secure the release of New England captives and Stevens went on missions in 1749, 1751, and 1752. A son, Enos, was captured near Fort Number Four in 1749—witnesses "saw the Indians lead off your son Enos, who was riding the mare, and lift him over the fence, so that we hope he is well"—but released before his father embarked on his first mission to Canada.

Phineas Stevens married his cousin, Elizabeth Stevens of Petersham, and had six children. He died in April 1756 at Chenecto, Nova Scotia, during the Seven Years' War.

[Coleman, *New England Captives Carried to Canada* 2: 151–54; Colin G. Calloway, ed., *Dawnland Encounters: Indians and Europeans in Northern New England* (Hanover: University Press of New England, 1991), 121–26; Calloway, *The Western Abenakis of Vermont, 1600–1800: War, Migration and the Survival of an Indian People* (Norman: University of Oklahoma Press, 1990), 117, 154–57, 160–64; Massachusetts Historical Society, Boston, Belknap Manuscripts 161A: 40.]

Journal of Capt. Phineas Stevens to and from Canada, 1749

PROVINCE OF THE MASSACHUSETTS BAY.
To the Honorable SPENCER PHIPS, Esq., Commander-in-Chief in and over
His Majesty's Province, and to the Hon'ble His Majesty's Council
now met in Boston, 1749.

MAY IT please your honor and honors, by your special command to me, I now humbly present the following pages, a true journal and account of my travel to and from Canada, whither your honor and honors were pleased to send me, with an account of my conduct with respect to my trust, and the remarkable occurrences that happened; the reception I met with, and some remarks I made on my road to and from Montreal, &c.—Which is as follows:

August, 1749. Sometime in August last, I was appointed by the honorable commissioners (then appointed by the honorable court) to go to Canada as their pilot. I accordingly repaired to my post at No. 4, to get my affairs in order, and proposed to attend them. Just as I was prepared, I received a letter from the honorable John Chandler, Esq., informing that the commissioners were not to go. Upon the receipt of which, I, with all speed, repaired to the honorable Col. Chandler, and from thence, by his direction, to Boston, where I received His Excellency Gov. Shirley's letter to the Governor of Canada, as also His Excellency and your honor's orders to proceed with the same to the Governor of Canada. September 13, I set out from Boston. Sept. 16, I arrived at Hadley, where I met my son, returned from his captivity. Sept. 17, Sabbath day at Hadley. Sept. 18, proceeded to Deerfield, to engage sergeant Hawks to go with me, according to order; but he declining to go, Sept. 20, I set out for No. 4, and lodged at Fort Dummer. Sept. 21, arrived at No. 4, where I remained until Sept. 26, when I took with me ensign John Burke of my company, instead of Hawks, and set out for Canada. That night lodged at Fort Dummer. Sept. 27, to Deerfield; 28, to Hadley; 29, tarried for the finishing of my clothes I had making there; 30, to Westfield; October 1, Sabbath day; 2, to town called No. 1; 3, to Canter Hook [Kinderhook?] 4, to Albany; 5 and 6, at Albany, preparing for our journey; 7, having agreed with four of the Cagnawaugon Mohawks to conduct us and carry our baggage to Canada, we proceeded on our journey, went five miles up Hudson's river, and lodged at a Dutch house; 8, proceeded with our canoes 11 miles, to a Dutch house, rebuilt since the war; 9, the water being very low, we hired our loading carried four miles by land to Stillwater, then with our canoes proceeded to Saratoga,—20 miles this day; 10, went up the river eight miles, and lodged aboard; 11, up the river four miles, and come to the carrying place over to Wood-Creek,—being foul weather, we tarried in a house newly built by Col. Lydias and Mr. Vander Haydon; 12, came to the upper carrying place, eight miles. This day, we met the Dutch ambassadors from Canada, who had with them two of our prisoners, and were refused any more of ours or theirs, under pretence made by the Indians that the province of the Massachusetts had a number of St. Francois Indians under confinement in Boston. There was also in company with them a Frenchman and Indian, coming to Boston by way of New-York, to know the truth of it.

October 13. Travelled eight miles in the carrying place with our canoes, baggage, &c.; 14, four miles to the lake St. Sacrament, and proceeded on said lake in our canoes, twelve miles and camped. This day we saw on the side of the lake St. Sacrament wigwams of St. Francois Indians, who appeared friendly, and one of my old acquaintance presented me with two wild geese. Oct. 15, sailed twelve miles on said lake—came to a wigwam of French Mohawks; they being acquaintance of our conductors, we could get no further this day. Oct. 16, sailed twenty miles, which brought us over said lake, and one mile down a small river to a carrying place, where we lodged; 17, carried our things one mile then down said river with our canoes to the drowned lands—then ten miles, and lodged; 18, it snowed, we lay still; 19, sailed five miles in our canoes and came to Crown Point, where we were kindly received and handsomely treated; but the commandant refused to let us go any further till the arrival of their sloop, which he expected in a short time, with which he expected orders to stop all that should come from New-England. The vessel coming that night, and bringing no such orders, (Oct. 20) after dinner the commandant gave us liberty to proceed on our journey. Bad weather and contrary winds retarding us, we did not arrive at St. John's, on Shamblee river, until the 26th, which is a large fort, mostly of timber, about twelve miles above Shamblee fort. At St. John's is the place where they load their vessels in order to supply Crown Point. At this fort, the commandant absolutely refused our proceeding, until he had orders from the Governor of Montreal. The officer sent one of our Indian company to Montreal with a letter. Oct. 27, continued at said fort; 28, having a convenient opportunity by a cart going to Lapperary, the commandant gave leave we should go forward; but if we met counter orders, to return. About half way, we met a Frenchman with horses from the Governor to fetch us;—we came to Lapperary a little before night, which is from St. John's fifteen miles.

In travelling this fifteen miles, I observed the vast labor and pains taking to make a passable road from St. John's to Lapperary—twelve miles of which was a very miry swamp, full of timber. They have cut the road two rods wide—they have made a causeway with timber—dug a trench on each side, which earth covers the timber: the land being so very wet, they are obliged to dig a number of drains from these trenches to great distances, taking all advantage of every fall of ground and run of water. This road is not yet quite completed: when finished, it will be a very good level way, and will render the supplying of Crown Point much easier than by the former way of Shamblee.

After we had refreshed ourselves, the ferryman told us he had orders to carry us immediately that night to Montreal. We directly set off, and arrived at the governor's about eight o'clock, it being nine miles by water. The governor received us very kindly—asked us to sup with him, which accordingly I did. The governor told me he should ask me no questions that night.

Oct. 29. Waited upon the governor that morning, who interrogated me very particular what was my business. I delivered the public letter, when he demanded of me all the private letters. He understanding that I had no special orders to treat with the governor-general, told me he thought it not proper I should go to Quebec, and that he would send the letter by an express; and if the governor-general thought it necessary, he would send for me; if not, I might expect, upon the return of the express, to be sent immediately home;—at the same time, he strictly forbid my having any conversation with the Indians,—and threatened, if he perceived I had, I should be immediately confined. Gave orders to my landlord, the King's interpreter, to keep us always under his inspection.

I continued at Montreal eight days, (where I was very well entertained.) I made it my constant business to inquire after prisoners: could hear of but three English from our parts, viz. Daniel Eaton, son to the widow Eaton, of Brunswick, now at Quebec, in the hands of the French; also a small boy, named John, alias Jonathan Door, taken from Rochester, in New-Hampshire, now in the hands of the St. Francois Indians; and a small girl, daughter to the widow Forster, of Casco Bay. She is now kept at Three Rivers, but belongs to a gentleman at Montreal, who designs her for the nunnery. There is also a number of Indians belonging to Cape Cod, two of which I saw at Montreal sold for slaves, who were very uneasy, and take it very hard that they are not treated as the rest of King George's subjects. There are two more with the St. Francois Indians; one of them I saw at Crown Point, who has married one of their squaws, and has no desire to come home,—he told me his name was Isaac Peck. The other I did not see. There is [are] more in the country, but could not find out where they lived.

While at Montreal, I was informed by a Dutch prisoner from Quebec, named David Abeall, who came home with me, that he saw two sloops loading with Indian stores, such as sleighs, snowshoes, &c., suitable for a winter's expedition, and, as he well understood the French language, he accidentally discovered they were designed for Chebucto.

Nov. 5. The express returned to Montreal with the answer to Gov. Shirley's letter. The 6th of November I was ordered home. I desired liberty to tarry one day longer; the governor told me the orders from the governor-general was so strict he could not grant me the favor. I accordingly set out with an officer and five soldiers, who had orders to bring us to Crown Point. Lodged at Lapperary that night.

As to Montreal, it is encompassed by a wall, and entrenched on the land side; a wall about 18 feet high from the bottom of the trench, which is about 8 feet deep and 16 wide; the wall 18 feet high on the water side, and no trench. The main battery is in the north-westerly corner of the city, on a rise of land which overlooks the wall all round. About 60 rods westward of the city there is a rise of land higher than the top of the walls.

Nov. 7, to Shamblee fort, where we were handsomely treated by the commandant; 8, to St. John's, twelve miles; 9, went on board a large batteau. As I have above, I here note, that at the emptying of the lake into Shamblee river there is a wind-mill, built of stone; it stands on the east side of the water, and several houses on both sides built before the war, but one inhabited at present. This day we came with our oars about forty miles—turned up a stream on the west side of the lake about one mile, where there was an officer with near 100 men cutting ship timber. The officer had a comfortable house—the men, barracks to live in. Here we lodged. Nov. 10, we came to an island in the lake and lodged; 11 and 12, lay wind-bound; 13, to Crown Point; 14, tarried at Crown Point. Being now left to care for ourselves, I hired two Cagnawaugen Indians to assist us as far as Col. Lydias' house, at the carrying place to Wood-Creek. As to Crown Point, it is a large stone fort, I judge about 12 or 14 rods square, of which I conclude your honors have often had

a description; I therefore beg leave only to note down some things in
respect to the citadel within said fort,—as that, it lies entirely distinct
from the wall of the fort, I passing entirely around it. It is four stories
high, each story contains four convenient rooms; the partitions are walls
of stone of great thickness; each story arched over with stone of great
thickness, for its twenty-four large stone steps from one story to another; each room has one very large window, three or four feet wide,
seven or eight high. The commandant lives in the third story, where there
are two such windows. In his room, I saw 110 small arms, 50 of them
fixed with bayonets, and about 50 pairs of pistols. I had not opportunity
to discover the number of cannon in the fort and citadel. The hill, often
spoke of, westerly of the fort, I judge to be not above forty rods distant,
and considerable higher than the top of the wall. I would here further
note, there are eighteen houses near Crown Point, some on each side of
the water, but not all inhabited at present.

Nov. 15. Took our departure with the Indians in a birch canoe—
came about five miles—found so much ice we could go no further;—
16, 17 and 18, lodged here, waiting for the ice being strong enough to
bear us; 19, drew our canoe on the ice—about seven miles found it very
difficult—falling several times into the water;—20, drew our canoe
three miles further on the ice—found it so weak we could not travel;
21, lay still; 22, travelled on the ice, leaving our canoe; 23, passed by
the mouth of Wood-Creek into a large pond, which has a small com-
munication to the drowned lands, lying to the west of the mouth of
Wood-Creek;—24, travelled over said pond about four or five miles in
length, and then two or three miles up a small river;—we here took our
packs on our backs and travelled in an Indian path, trodden by them in
their descents upon the Dutch this last war, and not before; nevertheless,
it's so trod that we could easily follow it, although the snow was four
or five inches deep. Nov. 25, we travelled in said road; 26, we came to
Hudson's river in the morning, about five miles above Col. Lydias' trading house. This carrying place, from where we first took up our packs,
I judge to be 22 miles to Hudson's river; the travelling level and exceeding good, except about two miles when we first left the aforesaid
small river. The course of this carrying place is N. and S. We came to
Lydias' trading house this day, where I had a convenient opportunity to
converse with the Cagnawaugen Indians by the help of Col. Lydias' son,
who could speak the language well. Four of them being present, they
manifested a great desire to live in peace, and said they should be very
glad to have opportunity to let the English know it. I told them it was
their own fault, or they might have continued in peace; however, not-

withstanding their breach of former covenants, if they come to the English to seek their favor, I doubted not but that our rulers would receive them, and make them welcome. I told them I was desired by some of our rulers to invite them to Boston; and further told them, notwithstanding the prohibition of the French Governor while I was in Canada, I now, being out of his reach, embraced this opportunity to send them a belt of wampum, to be delivered to their Chiefs, desiring them to come to Boston; saying to them, if your Chiefs, upon receiving this belt, shall be disposed to come, they may come by Albany or No. 4; if they come by the way of Albany, Col. Lydias will take care to conduct them; if by the way of No. 4, I will take care to conduct them to the Governor. They received the belt and message cheerfully, and promised to deliver them both faithfully.

Nov. 27. I left Col. Lydias' house, and made the best speed hither. Dec. 11. I arrived at Cambridge, and delivered the letter to your honor.

The foregoing is humbly submitted by your honor and honors' most dutiful and most obedient servant,

Boston, Dec. 15, 1749.   PHINEAS STEVENS.

[from *Collections of the New Hampshire Historical Society* vol. 5 (Concord: Asa McFarland, 1837), 199–205.]

Journal of Captain Phineas Stevens' Journey to Canada, 1752

Instructions to Capt. Phineas Stevens and Mr. Nathaniel Wheelwright, appointed to
proceed to Canada, to negotiate the restoration of the Captives belonging to this
Province, now remaining in the hands of the French or Indians there

You ARE hereby directed with all convenient speed to proceed to Albany, and there furnishing yourselves with a suitable Guide and Guides and other Assistance necessary for your convenient and safe Travel, to go direct to the Fort at Crown Point, and upon your arrival there apply yourselves to the Commanding Officer of that Garrison, and after shewing him your Passport and acquainting him with your general business, request of him to give Orders for your Speedy and Safe Conveyance to the Governour or Commander in Chief of the Province of Canada.

And upon your arrival at the place of Residence of the said Commander-in-Chief, immediately wait on him, and deliver my Letter to him shew him your Passport, and take his time for receiving his Answer to my demand of his delivering up, without Ransom, the Captives in the hands of the French or Indians; which you are to urge as far as you shall find necessary, or Convenient.

But if you find he cannot be prevailed with to release the Captives without Ransom, you must treat with him about their release upon the easiest and most reasonable Terms that may be obtained.

You must use all the advantages you may have of getting a knowledge of the several Prisoners, whether English or Indians belonging to this Province, now remaining in that Country, with their respective Circumstances and Condition, and if it should be pretended that any of them are unwilling to return you must endeavour, if it be possible to come at a Speech with them, and use your best endeavours to prevail upon them to return with you, with the leave of the Governour or Commander-in-Chief.

You are hereby impowered and directed to draw upon the Province Treasurer, for such sum or sums as you may find necessary, as well for the Ransome of the Prisoners, as for the Charge of their Travel and other Contingencies that may require it, or use such other way or method of supplying your Credit as you may find most suitable.

When your business is finished and you have received the Governour of Canada's Despatches for this Government, take back your English Passport and get one from the French Governour for your safe conduct home.

You must keep a Journal of your Proceedings, and also an Account of the Articles of Expense of the Publick money put into your hands, and lay the same before me and the Council, at your return.

Camb[rid]g[e] April the 15th 1752.   S. PHIPS.

                                          [Cambrg N.E., April 14, 1752.

Sir [The Governor of Canada],

This comes to your Excellency by Captain Phineas Stevens, who was employed by Governour Shirley,'before his departure for Great Britain, to carry Dispatches to you.

The Affair Captain Stevens was then engaged in (viz. to procure the recovery and return of our Captives in the hands of the French and Indians) being not yet fully effected, I have sent him together with Mr. Nathaniel Wheelwright, with these my Letters to you: And with Directions to do every thing necessary on the part of this Government, for the Deliverance of the rest of your Captives, still remaining in any part of the Government of Canada.

You will therefore please to receive these Gentlemen in the Character of Messengers from this Government, for transacting the Affair above-mentioned, and give them all the assistance necessary to make their Business successfull, that so, (if it be possible) there may not remain one single subject of This His Majesty's Government, either English or Indian under their miserable Captivity.

And I am the rather moved to urge this Business with freedom and importunity, by reason of the solicitous care our respective Masters have expressed to have this matter completely effected; as you will see by the inclosed Copy of his Most Christian Majesty's Order to your Excellency (which I suppose you have received), the Counterpart of which I have also received from his Britannick Majesty, my most Gracious Master; and I have so completely fulfilled the Directions contained therein, as that I am well assured that there is not one single Person, French or Indian, Subject of his Most Catholick Majesty, or in alliance with him, under Captivity, in any part of this Government.

I must in a particular manner repeat my pressing Demands for the restoration of any of those Indians, (now surviving) the Subjects of this his Majesty's Government, who were taken upon the Sea, being on a Whaling Voyage, or any other Indians belonging to this Province, some of whom it has been reported are treated as Slaves, tho' in this Province they live in as much freedom as the English themselves.

It seems highly unjust and contrary to the Form of the Articles of Peace, always stipulated between the Powers of Europe, that this Government should be put to any charge for the Ransom of Prisoners of War, after a Peace concluded; and I am confident that no one instance can be produced of any Ransom being paid by the French Government or private persons for the release of their Prisoners or that their Release was ever denied them under pretence of their being in the hands of the Indians: And therefore I must once more urge my Demand that all the Prisoners belonging to this Government may be discharged without Ransom.

I have [*remainder of this letter missing*]

April 27, 1752. I set out from No. 4. for Canada, my son Samuel with me; came two miles below Fort Turner; and lodged at Caleb Hows.

April 28th. Hired said How with two horses (for which I paid him two dollars) came to Deerfield. Lodged at Col. Hinsdell's.

April 29th. To Hatfield, where I met with Mr. Wheelwright, and returned with him to Deerfield the same day, where we remained, preparing for our journey till

May 4th then set out and came at Francis Taylor's, 12 miles, and lodged for 1 dollar.

May 5th. To Fort Massachusetts, accompanied by Capt. Moses.

May 6th. After making a present to the soldiers of one dollar, we set out, accompanied by Capt. Williamson, till noon; then took our leave of him, and came to Albany. Same day had an account of three soldiers being drowned in the morning of the said day, belonging to the fort at Albany.

May 7th we spent in visiting and consulting with some of the chief men in the place how to proceed in our Journey to Canada.

May 8th. We agreed with an Indian to assist with his son in our journey; and also engaged Mr. Sanders (the mayor of the city) to provide all things needful for our journey.

May 9th. We sent a man to Skanately to buy a canoe, for a suitable one was not to be found in Albany.

May 10th. Lords Day—exceeding dry sermon.

May 11th. The two Indians came from Stockbridge, in order to go with us.

May 12th. Fixed our canoe, and set all things in readiness for our journey.

May 13th. I set out from Albany, with Heywood, and Samuel; and the two Indians came with our canoe and lading 16 miles, and lodged at Jacob Foot's, a Dutchman.

May 14th. I hired the said Dutchman to carry our baggage in a wagon to Stillwater, 6 miles. I with the two Indians came up the swift water in the canoe. Then took the lading and came to Saratogue and lodged [having travelled] 24 miles this day. Mr. Wheelwright came on horseback this day from Albany, and lodged at Saratogue.

May 15th. I came with the canoe three miles above Lydies'es, and lodged at the foot of the falls. Mr. Wheelwright lodged at Lydies'es. It rained at night.

May 16th. Col. Lydies joined Mr. Wheelwright and met the canoe (at the place where we take our departure from Hulstines [or Hulstions] river) with five horses which assisted us in carrying our baggage. We came this day half way over the carrying place, and lodged by the branch of Wood creek. It rained hard at night.

May 17th. We came to the Lake St. Sacrement about noon, with all our bagg[ag]e. Col. Lydies, with the two Indians with him, turned back. After we had mended our canoe, we embarked, and came eight miles, and camped on the west side of the lake. Showery weather.

May 18th. Came over said lake. Lodged at the canoeing place from said lake to the drowned land.

May 19th. Carried our baggage over the carrying place; then embarked, and came to the French settlements, three miles south of Crown Point. Lodged in a French house. A very stormy day. Wind at head, and rain.

May 20th. The storm continued at North East and rained. We came to Crown Point at two o'clock afternoon. The commandant received us kindly.

May 21st. It stormed. We remained at the Fort.

May 22d. The storm somewhat abated. We set off from the Fort at six afternoon in a large batteau accompanied by a French officer and five soldiers; came about two miles, and lodged on the east side of the lake in a French house.

N.B. The commandant of the Fort fitted us out with all things necessary for our journey.

May 23d. Set out very early in the morning. Cloudy and some rain;

but not much wind. Came about thirty miles; the wind freshened up at northeast. We put into the mouth of a river, on the west side of the lake; at which place there is a fine pine plain. After we had refreshed ourselves, we embarked and came twelve miles, and lodged on an island.

May 24th. Lords day. The wind blew up at south. We hoisted sail at day light. The wind continued in our favor till afternoon, which brought us in sight of Fort La Motte; then turned into the northeast. We then took down our sail, and rowed till four afternoon, which brought us to the south end of the above said island, in sight of a number of French houses; but the wind so very high, and having a large bay to cross, we turned to the west shore. A little before night the wind fell: We crossed the bay three miles to a French house and lodged.

May 25th. Set forward early in the morning. Came fifteen miles, and stopped at a French house on the east side, just above an Island. Below said Island it is called Chamblee River. Here we refreshed ourselves, etc. Then embarked, and came eighteen miles to St. Johns fort. Immediately upon our arrival the officer of the fort sent an express to La Prarie for horses and carts to convey our baggage from hence.

May 26th. About ten in the morning the two carts came. After dinner loaded our things into the carts and came off. The officer, Mr. Wheelwright, and myself rode on horses sent for that purpose. Came to La Prarie a little before night. It rained most of the way.

May 27th. A large batteau and a number of hands was made ready, which brought us to Montreal. We arrived at the Governor's about ten in the forenoon. After he had read our passport, letters, etc., we retired to Madam Carols where we took up our lodgings; then returned to the Governor's, and dined. After this we visited the commissioners and several other gentlemen.

May 28th and so [continued doing] till *the*
30th [which] we spent in making the best inquiries we could where our prisoners were, etc.

May 31st. The Sabbath day. It rained at night.

June the 1st. We dined with the Governor, and at night supped with an officer. This day a schooner arrived from Quebec, and we have a hint as if she brings news of a large army's being about to go to Jebuctoo and also that a mutiny has happened amongst the soldiers at Quebec.

June 2d. Had the news of the Indians killing and taking four of our people.

June 3d. Dined with the Commissary.

June 4th. Mr. Linglauesne and his wife came to visit us.

June 5th. Nothing remarkable.

June 6th. Mr. Wheelwright and I wrote a letter to Governor Phips, and several other letters for New England.

June 7th. Sabbath day. Very hot weather.

June 8th. Mr. Wheelwright went to Connewago with a number of French gentlemen.

June 9th. Had further news of more mischief being done on our people, and that three prisoners were brought to Crown Point.

June 10th. Paid a visit to the Governor, who told us he had no intelligence of any prisoner being brought to Crown Point. At night we supped at Mr. St. Luke Laurens. This day three men and a woman obtained a pass from the Governor and set out for New England themselves. Said the[y] belonged to the Province of Pennsylvania.

June 11th. Nothing remarkable.

June 12th. I visited French's sisters. This day were told by John Tasble that the mischief the Indians had done on the English was at White River, and that there was six in company. Two made their escape; two killed; and two taken prisoners. At night was taken with a terrible purging.

June 13th. I kept house with the same distemper.

June 14th. Sabbath day. Two small schooners arrived at Montreal from Quebec, loaded with flour; which might certainly denote a very great scarcity; for the most of the supply for that place are in time of plenty carried from hence. This day dined at Madam Lestushes Supped at a gentleman's house near the same place.

June 15th. Lewse, a Frenchman, (who lately came from Albany,) came to visit us. Gave an account of two negroes being taken at a place called Canterbury on Merrimac River; one of which he saw at Crown Point, bought by the Commissary of said Fort, for 400 Livres. The other made his escape the fortnight after he was taken. He also informed us he saw nine Indians set off from thence for war, who told him they designed for some of the English settlements, for if they must fight the English they would not go so far. They look upon them to be all one people.

June 16th. It thundered and rained a small matter in the morning. Mr. Wheelwright set off for Quebec about 12 o'clock, with Mr. Deplace, the high Sheriff. We have repeated accounts of the Dureedweer Indians doing [evil] upon the French traders in the westward, which puts the merchants in Montreal into a consternation. There is nothing can hurt this country so much as to distress their trade in those parts;

for their income from thence seems to be the dependance of the whole country. Vast numbers are employed in that business. We are told that 200 large birch canoes and batteaux are gone up the river this spring—some five, and some six men each; so that upwards of a thousand men are already gone upon that business. Their method of carrying on the trade is for the chief traders of factors to remain in that country for three or four years, and have supplies sent them yearly. Tis said some of these traders go 3000 miles; but their supplies are not sent so far—they go no farther than some of the French forts that are kept in those parts—viz—those westward parts. So these ramblers are obliged to return once a year to said forts for a new supply. Could our people be so well spirited in time of war as to go and destroy those forts, it must in a short time so impoverish Canada that it must fall an easy prey into our hands.

June 17th. A soldier was shot to death for deserting from some of the French forts in the westward. This day I received a letter from Mr. Hardwick, a prisoner at St. Francois, taken from Chebucto.

June 18th. It thundered and rained a small matter, but the drought is very great. The wheat in this country suffers very much. There is intelligence from Quebec that several vessels are arrived there from France laden with flour and pork.

June 19th. I received a letter from the missionary of St. Francis and another from the abovementioned woman. A number of Indians came to town tonight. Tis said they have brought two scalps, and two prisoners; but it wants confirmation.

June 20th. I went round the town to look for a good gun. The scalps abovementioned were brought from the westward, and tis said are Indian's scalps.

June 21st. Sabbath day. Hot and dry.

June 22d. A number of the chiefs of the St. Francois Indians came to Montreal, and showed me the respect as to come the same day and pay me a visit.

June 23d. After dinner the Governor sent for me to appear before him and his council to receive a message from the St. Francois Indians. I accordingly did and after their spokesman had made his speech, he delivered me a large belt of wampum, which he said I must deliver with his message to the Governor at Boston. The same day I gave my old Indian father a hat, price 10 Livres—he being one of the chiefs abovementioned.

June 24th. I sent a letter to one of the Jesuits at St. Francois by an Indian.

June 25th. I had a hint from an Indian as if a belt of wampum was come into this country from some of the Six Nations in order for a treaty with some or all the tribes of Indians here. There is numbers of of the former tribes of Indians coming to Montreal every few days. The drought is now very extraordinary. The wheat in this country, tis thought, has received so much damage already that a crop cannot be expected this year, and as they had but a very small crop last year, the calamity of this country must certainly in a little time be very great.

June 26th. Something likely for rain, but very hot and dry.

June 27th. A small matter of rain fell in the morning; in the afternoon windy and dry. The great probability of a scarcity casts a sadness in all faces. In the evening it clouded up and bid fair for rain, but broke away with but a small sprinkling.

June 28th. Sabbath day, and kept as a day of rejoicing with them for the birth of a young prince born in France, they have lately had news of. They went in procession and fired all their cannon, viz. 33 in number. A black cloud came up at night, but no rain.

June 29th. I paid my respects to the Governor. He informed me of a great difficulty at Chebucto, but did not let me know what it was about.

June 30th. Four large birch canoes containing nine or ten Indians each came to Montreal. Tis said those Indians' place of abode is 1800 miles from hence. There came also a batteau with nine or ten Frenchmen to town from a French fort west of our English governments, 900 miles from hence. They brought with them an Englishman, who deserted from some of our Indian traders from Philadelphia. His name is Jonathan Lafavour. There came also four canoes of Indians from Albany.

July 1st. A large number of Indians came to town from Becanco[ur] an Indian town on the south side the Great River near the Three Rivers. This day a number of women came to the Commissary for bread, and upon his refusing to let them have any, one of them took him by the throat. Exceeding hot and dry weather.

July 2d. I received a letter from Mr. Wheelwright at Quebec informing of his speedy arrival at Montreal. The weather is yet exceeding hot.

July 3d. Mr. Wheelwright returned to Montreal from Quebec; brought with him two men taken at New Meadows last summer. Great numbers of Indians are daily coming to town to receive their presents from their fathers, as they term it.

July 4th. Two of the Ottawa Indians, being almost drunk, fell out to such a degree that one stabbed the other with his knife so that he expired in a few minutes. An old Indian that sit by and see the action ordered a lad of about 14 or 15 years of age (being a near relation of him that was stabbed) to charge his gun and be ready to kill the other as soon as the first was dead. The boy accordingly did with deliberation. The French people that were by told the murderer to make his escape. He moved off slowly. The boy stood with his gun in his hand till his kinsman was quite gone; and as soon as he see him fetch his last breath, he went after the other with as much calmness as he was in pursuit of some game. When the murderer saw the lad after him he endeavored to hide himself; but the boy was so lucky as to see him lie down in a place of wheat. The boy went as near as he thought convenient, and then first gave him a mortal wound; but he retained so much strength that he rose up and pursued the boy but not far. The old Indian that gave the boy his orders seeing that he was not killed outright ran with his knife and gave him several stabs, so that he died immediately—so that in half an hour's time they were both dead. This was transacted just without the wall of Montreal.

July 5th. Sunday. Two prisoners were brought to town from St. Francoes, viz. Seth Webb and Amos Eastman. We bought them at 300 Livres each, and ten livres each for the charge of bringing them to Montreal.

July 6th. I received a letter from the missionary of St. Franscoes.

July 7th. Mrs. Honor Hancok, a prisoner taken from Jebucto was brought to Montreal; which we bought at 300 livres, and 30 livres for the charge of bringing her.

July 8th. Mr. Wheelwright and I went to visit a captive girl named Elizabeth Cody. She lived at the hospital south of the town.

July 9th. A great number of the St. Franscoes Indians came to Montreal. Brought with them some of our captive boys. There came up a smart thunder shower at night, and for about half an hour it rained hard, so that the water run in brooks in the streets.

July 10th. Mr. Wheelwright and I paid our respects to the Governor, in the morning. [In the] Afternoon I bought two guns, price 65 livres, 10 sous, each; of which Mr. Wheelwright paid 66 livres, 15 sous. The heat increases very much.

July 11th. An exceedingly hot day. Being by the river side I see the French people dig ice out of the bank, which was hove up in the winter and covered by the bank falling down upon it. They use this ice to preserve their fresh meat.

July 12th. Sabbath day. Hot and dry. Clouds of smoke are rising in all parts of this country—a surprising sight at this time of year.

July 13th. Mr. Wheelwright and my self went before the Governor with a Dutch girl taken in the war, named Elizabeth Cody, and an English boy named Solomon Metchel, 12 years old taken about one year ago. Upon their refusing to go home the Governor would not give them up. The same day John Starks was brought to Montreal by his Indian Master. He was taken a hunting this spring. He is given us for an Indian poney in his place, for which we paid 515 livres.

July 14th. We took our leave of the Governor and the rest of the chief Officers and made all things ready for our return to New England.

July 15th. We set out from Montreal for New England. Brought with us eight prisoners, viz: two taken from Jebucto, Thomas Stanard and Honor Hancock; two men from New Hampshire, Amos Estmon and John Stark, taken a hunting; Joseph Fortner, taken west of Pennsylvania; from the Massachusetts Edmund Hinckley, Samuel Lambart, and Seth Webb. We came this day to Laperary. It rained a smart shower as we crossed the river, and some in the night.

July 16th. Set out from thence—came to St. Johns. Our baggage was brought in carts. An officer is sent with us, who has orders to conduct us to the first English land. We remained till 5 afternoon, then set out with a batteau and a birch canoe. Came 18 miles and lodged.

July 17th. Embarked very early in the morning. Came about 4 miles. Met several canoes from Albany. It rained some showers.

July 12th. Sabbath day. Two small barks arrived from Quebec. I this day saw a man in prison. [He said] His name was Johnson and that he had an uncle in Boston, named George Johnson, and a kinsman one Wm. Johnson. His father, he says, lives in Edinburgh in Scotland, and is a man of note. Look back for the 12th day and then add this above.

July 18th. Embarked early in the morning—wind at head and some rain. We came to the mouth of Otter creek and turned ashore to lodge; but the small flies were so plenty that we could not sleep. We embarked again about 2 at night—wind at northeast and some hard showers of rain. We hoisted sail and came to Crown Point about sunrise. I would note that my old Indian master came in the canoe with me and that the quarter part of the St. Fransioes Indians have left their town for want of protection, and are on the road to the Dutch Settlements. We remained at Crown Point all day, being Sabbath day. The wind blew hard all the day, but we could not prevail with the Indians, being none here but of the St. Fransioes tribe. The negro which the Commissary of the fort bought of the Indian taken at Canterbury, we cannot get for the same money we suppose he bought him for. The gentleman declares he gave 600 livres for him. We have been informed he gave but 400—the captain's lady told us she was offered him for that money.

July 20th. The Indians we had engaged to go with us to Lydies's failing us and not coming, obliged us to remain at the fort all day. Just at night agreed with two other Indians so that Mr. Wheelwright and five of our people set off at sunset. I with the rest lodged at the fort.

July 21st. I, with the people left with me, set out from Crown Point at ten in the morning, accompanied by an officer and ten soldiers, who brought us in two log canoes. We came all night up the drowned land. Arrived at the landing place at the west end of the great bay west of the mouth of wood creek. At 8 the next morning we slept and refreshed ourselves till two afternoon; then bound up our packs and set forward. Came about one mile and passed by a family of Indians. Came 7 miles and camped.

July 23d. In the mo[r]ning I missed my sword which I had left at the place where we first took up our packs. Sent two men back: they found it with the Indians abovementioned. We came this day to Col. Lydis's. Met with Mr. Wheelwright (who came by the way of the lake St. Sacrement.) He was obliged to leave the canoe and loading on the carrying place. The Indians leaving him, he came to Lydeses for help.

July 24th. I went with Lydieses son with three horses to assist in getting our things to Hutson's River. I hired two Mohawks to carry the canoe. Brought our things to the river and returned to Lydyes at night met great numbers of the St. Francois Indians coming to Albany with beaver.

July 25th. Came from Lydyeses to Saratogue. Lodged at Mr. Killians. The two Mohawks that brought our canoe over the carrying came thus far with us for which we paid them six dollars.

July 26th. Sabbath day. Mr. Wheelwright and his man came on horseback to Albany. I with the canoe and the rest of our people came within 10 miles of Albany. I paid 3 dollars for the carrying our things by the bad water.

July 27th. Came to Albany about 12 o'clock. Remained there the rest of the day.

July 28th. I remained at Albany upon the desire of a number of the St. Francois Indians, who this day had a sort of treaty with the Dutch Traders. They met at 10 forenoon—[They] made a small speech to the Dutch, in which they manifest a great desire for peace; then delivered a belt of wampum and a pack of beaver. The Dutch desired their attendance at 3 afternoon. They accordingly met, when the Dutch made their speech, in which they gave them free liberty to come and trade without molestation, and [told them] that the road was open. Then [the Dutch] made them a present of a belt of wampum, and two pieces of ——— 2 kegs of rum, tobacco, etc. The Indians received them thankfully.

July 29th. I set out from Albany with my son. Came to the first Dutch house on Hoosack river, and lodged. Wm. Heywood and the seven prisoners who came off the day before lodged at Fort Massachusetts.

July 30th. I came to Capt. Rice's where I overtook the above said men. Here we all lodged.

July 31st. Came to Deerfield and lodged.

August 1st. I sent an express to Boston with the letters that came from Canada; and four of the prisoners went down the country road for home, three of which belonged to the eastward, the others to Jebucto. I came with the rest of the people to Northfield.

August 2d. Lord's day. Went to meeting. After meeting came to Hinsdell's Fort with my son and Joseph Fortner. The two Hampshire men set off for Wenchester.

August 3d. Came with my son to No. 2. Left Fortner with Col. Hinsdell. Wm. Heywood remains at Northfield to hunt for his horse, that left him at the carrying place.

August 4th. Came to No. 4. Found my family all well, my wheat all reaped, etc.

August 5th and *6th.* My people finished reaping my oats.

August 7th. I begun to ——— them.

August 8th. A paper was drew up, and signed for me to go to New Hampshire, etc.

August 9th. Lords day.

August 10th. A day of rain. I prepared for my Journey.

August 11th. I set out for Portsmouth. Came to Col. Hinsdells fort.

August 12th. Stopped the greater part of day at said fort to get my linen washed. Came to Northfield at night.

August. 13th. [Came] to Deerfield to get my clothes. Returned the same day to Winchester, where I met Capt. Hubard. We lodged at Major Willards.

August 14th. We came to ——— and lodged at Col. Berrys house. It rained the most of the day.

August 15th. [Came] to Luneinburge.

August 16th. Lords day.

August 17th. Hubard and I, in company with Mr. Bellows came to Col. Blanchard at Dunstable and lodged.

August 18th. After dinner I set out from thence and came to Chester and lodged at Capt. Dalford's.

August 19th. Said Capt. set out with me and came to Portsmouth. I remained there till *the*

24th. In which time I lodged a proposition with the Governor and counsel for the township No. 4. I came from Portsmouth to Ipswich, and lodged at Mr. Rogers'.

August 25th. Came to Boston by the way of Cambridge and Roxbury.

August 26th. At Boston I lodged with Mr. Lyman.

27. I set out from Boston. Came as far as Marlborough.

August 28th. [Came] to Rutland.

August 29th. At Rutland.

August 30th. Lords day.

August 31st. Came from Rutland to Hardwicke.

Sept. 1st. Came to Hatfield.

Sept. 2nd. [Came] to Deerfield. Bought a trunk of Madame Hinsdell, in which I put my clothes and sent them to Northfield. The next day, which, according to act of Parliament, is *the*

14th. I came to Col. Hinsdells fort. It rained some.

Sept. 15th. I came to Killbruns at No. 3, and lodged.

Sept. 16th. [Came] home to No. 4.

Sept. 17th. Lords day. From *the*

18th to the *23d* exceeding dry weather. The Great River is thought to be as low as has been known these many years past. Some of our people are gone down to Deerfield and Hatfield this week, viz. Dr. Hastings and wife, Joseph Willards and Hastings wives. Thos. Putnam and Isaac Parker went with a canoe for salt, etc. I this week begun to fall timber for a house.

Sept. 24th. Sabbath day.

Sept. 25th. I sawed timber for clapboards etc. A great supply of rain at night. The water in puddles the next morning.

Sept. 26th. It rained part of the day.

Sept. 27th. A hard frost at night.

Sept. 28th. I began to make a road at the south end of my house lot. Ebr. Putnam and his brother Larence set out upon a journey.

Sept. 29th. I finished the above said road. The whole cost me seven days work.

Sept. 30th. It rained hard afternoon.

October 1st. Lords day. Stephen Farnsworth had an ox killed by the fall of a tree.

Oct. 2d. Wright had a barrel rum brought to the fort. I bought a three acre lot of Joseph Woods.

Oct. 3d. Elijah Grout left me and set out for home.

Oct. 4th. I fell timber, etc.

Oct. 5th. I begun to hew timber for my house.

Oct. 6th. I gathered my corn.

Oct. 7th. I carted my corn.

Oct. 8th. Sabbath day. It rained hard all day.

Oct. 9th. The storm continued.

Oct. 10th. At husking. Pleasant weather, but clouded up at night, and bid fair for more rain.

Oct. 11th. It rained the most of the day.

Oct. 12th. I finished husking my corn.

Oct. 13th. It rained part of the day. It is now a very wet season.

Oct. 14th. Lieut. Bellows came to No. 4.

Oct. 15th. Sabbath day.

Oct. 16th. I fell timber, etc.

Oct. 17th. Stephen Davis came to town.

Oct. 18th. I hewed timber with six scoope. The boat came to the falls with salt, rum, etc.

Oct. 19th. Hewed timber with 8 schooars.

Oct. 20th. Hewed with 6 do. Doct. Hastings and wife returned home. Ruth Parker came home.

Oct. 21st. Hewed with six hands.

Oct. 22d. Sabbath day.

Oct. 23d. Hewed with six do. Our people are yet busy at harvesting.

Oct. 24th. Five hands at hewing.

Oct. 25th. Five do. This day two barrels [of] rum [were] brought to the fort.

Oct. 26th. It rained hard the most of the day.

Oct. 27th. Four hands schooring. Drew part timber off.

Oct. 28th. I finished hewing in the forenoon. Three at schooring. Afternoon the carpenters went home.

Oct. 29th. Sabbath day.

Oct. 30th. I drew my hay out of the great meadow. Our cattle are now all let into said meadow.

Oct. 31st. There fell a small snow in the morning about 2 inches deep, but all went off before night.

Nov. 1st., 2d., and 3d. I drew timber for my house etc. Fine pleasant weather. We are now set out for ———

Nov. 4th. Fine weather.

Nov. 5th. Sabbath day, very warm for the season. I have a cow calf.

Nov. 6th. Drew timber, etc.

Nov. 7th. Davis came in the morning, father Perry with him. Began to frame my house the same day.

Nov. 8th. At framing. Deacon Addams and family came to No. 4.

Nov. 9th. At framing. Lieut. Johnson's wife brought abed of a daughter.

Nov. 10th. At framing. This day a number of men from Woodstock came to No. 4.

Nov. 11th. Forenoon it rained—obliged us to lie by. Afternoon at raising. Begun to raise the sides of the house.

Nov. 12th. Lords day. Our people begin to assemble together for the worship of God.

Nov. 13th. At framing. The lower part of the house is almost up.

Nov. 14th. At framing. A small snow fell at night.

Nov. 15th. I begun to raise my house.

Nov. 16th. I finished. Wheeler and old Mr. Putnam raised the same day. Davis and Jeremy went home.

Nov. 17th and *18th.* Nothing worth notice.

Nov. 19th. Lords day.

Nov. 20th. I sent my son Enos down to Hatfield in company with several others. A stormy day.

Nov. 21st. The storm continued.

Nov. 22d. I worked at my cellar.

August 10th 1752
Cash borrowed of John Hastings Jr 14 Spanish Dollars
                   of Caleb Wright   Do. 2
                   of Moses Wheeler   1 do.
After I returned home I paid John Hastings one dollar, and allowed Wright for his on my bond against him.

Nov. 23d. I went to No. 3 to help Lieut. Bellows raise his house and a barn. A small snow fell at night.

Nov. 24th. We finished raising the above buildings and returned home. Cold for the season.

A Short Description of the City of Montreal in Canada

Viz: Its built on the south side of the great island called the Island of Montreal. This island is said to be fifteen leagues in length and in breadth, called the most healthful part of their country, mostly inhabited by tenants put on by the priests and nuns; for they own the greater part of the land. The city is about ¾ of a mile in length, and about 100 rods wide in the widest place. It stands on the side of St. Lawrence's river, encompassed round with a wall 16 or 18 feet high. The wall on the river side stands about three rods from highwater mark. The town lies upon a descent of land, so that from the water side to the upper part, or northwestwardly side of [the] town, is up hill, but not very steep.

There is but two streets that go through the length of the town, and so about nine or ten cross streets. This town contains about four hundred dwelling houses, besides public buildings. There is five chapels or churches, viz: one for the barefoot friars; one for the close nuns, to which joins the hospital; one do. for the holy sisters, and one for the Jesuits; and one which is called the great church, where the priests say mass. There is one more just without the walls on the south side joining to the Kings Hospital.

N.B. The walls of the city are not so wide at the north end as at the south; for at the north are but about thirty rods wide. Here is the battery, on a rise of land which commands all the city.

[from Newton D. Mereness, ed., *Travels in the American Colonies* (New York: Macmillan, 1916), 302–22.]

SUSANNA AND
JAMES JOHNSON

The Johnson family was captured by Abenakis at Charlestown in August 1754. James Johnson had migrated from Ireland as a boy and settled on the New Hampshire frontier, marrying Susanna, one of twelve children of Moses and Susanna Willard. James and Susanna's children were Sylvanus (born in 1748), Susanna (1750), Mary, also called Polly (1752), who later married Colonel Timothy Bedel of Haverhill, New Hampshire, and Elizabeth Captive, born en route to captivity.

They were first taken to St. Francis, and their accounts provide a valuable picture of the Abenaki village, but as tensions and suspicions heightened in the Seven Years' War, they were moved to prison in Quebec, where they endured hardship, hunger and smallpox. A child born during imprisonment in Quebec lived only a few hours.

In 1757, Susanna Johnson, her sister, and two daughters were sent to England, exchanged for French prisoners, and returned to America. Susanna and James were reunited and returned to their old home in Lancaster, Massachusetts. James became a captain in the provincial army at Ticonderoga, where he was killed the following summer during General Abercrombie's assault on the French fortress.

Susanna returned to Charlestown, her father having been killed by Indians during her captivity. She married John Hastings in 1762, by whom she had seven more children, and died in 1810.

Told in the first person, Susanna Johnson's narrative was partly dictated by her and partly compiled from notes she and her husband made during their imprisonment. First printed in Walpole, New Hampshire, in 1796, it went through several subsequent editions.

[Coleman, New England Captives Carried to Canada 2: 302–303; Henry H. Saunderson, History of Charlestown, New Hampshire (Claremont, N.H., 1876).]

A Narrative of the Captivity of Mrs. Johnson

Notices of the Willard Family

To TRACE the progress of families from their origin to the present day, when, perhaps, they are spread over the four quarters of the globe, and no memorandums are found except in the uncertain pages of memory, is a task which can be but feebly performed. In noticing the name of Willard, which was my family name, I cannot pretend to accuracy; but the information which I have collected will, perhaps, be of some service to others who possess a greater stock; and if the various branches of families would contribute their mites, it would be an easy way of remedying the deficiency which at present exists in American genealogy.

The first person by the name of Willard who settled in this country was Major Willard, whose name is recorded in the history of New England wars. In the year 1675, in the time of "Philip's war," (a notorious Indian, who lived within the present limits of the State of Rhode Island), Major Willard, who then lived in the town of Lancaster, in Massachusetts, commanded a troop of horse; and among his vigorous services he relieved the town of Brookfield from the Nipnet Indians, who had burned every house but one, and had almost reduced that to capitulation. When Lancaster was destroyed by the Indians Major Willard removed to Salem, where he spent the rest of his days. He had two sons; one of whom was a settled minister in the town of Groton, from which place he was driven by the Indians, and was afterwards installed in Boston. His other son, Simon, established himself on Still River, since taken from Lancaster and incorporated into the town of Harvard. He had nine sons; Simon, Henry, Hezekiah, John, Joseph, Josiah, Samuel, Jonathan, and James. Josiah removed to Winchester, in New Hampshire, and afterwards commanded Fort Dummer; the rest inherited the substance of their father, and lived to very advanced ages in the vicinity of their birth. They all left numerous families, who spread over the United States. His eldest son, Simon, was my grandfather. He had two sons, Aaron and Moses: Aaron lived in Lancaster, and Moses, my father, removed to Lunenburg. I ought to remark, that my grandmother Willard, after the death of her husband, married a person by the name of Farnsworth, by whom she had three sons, who were the first settlers of Charlestown, No. 4. One of them was killed by the Indians.

My father had twelve children. He removed to Charlestown, No. 4, in 1742, and soon had the pleasure to find his children settled around him. He was killed by the Indians in 1756. My mother died in March, 1797, and had lived to see twelve children, ninety-two grandchildren, one hundred and twenty-three great-grandchildren, and four great-great-grandchildren. The whole that survive are now settled on Connecticut River.

Notices of Mr. James Johnson

In the year 1730 my great-uncle, Colonel Josiah Willard, while at Boston, was invited to take a walk on the Long Wharf to view some transports who had just landed from Ireland. A number of gentlemen present were viewing the exercise of some lads, who were placed on shore to exhibit their activity to those who wished to purchase. My uncle spied a boy of some vivacity, of about ten years of age, and who was the only one in the crew who spoke English. He bargained for him. I have never been able to learn the price; but as he was afterwards my husband, I am willing to suppose it a considerable sum. He questioned the boy respecting his parentage and descent. All the information he could get was, that young James, a considerable time previous, went to sea with his uncle, who commanded a ship and had the appearance of a man of property; that this uncle was taken sick at sea and died: immediately after his death they came in sight of this ship of Irish transports, and he was put on board. His being the only one of the crew who spoke English and other circumstances have led his friends to conclude that this removal on board the Irish ship was done to facilitate the sequestration of his uncle's property. He lived with Colonel Willard until he was twenty years old, and then bought the other year of his time. In 1748 Governor Shirley gave him a lieutenant's commission under Edward Hartwell, Esq.

Situation of the Country in 1744

It is an old maxim, that, after a man is in possession of a small, independent property, it is easy for him to acquire a great fortune. Just so with countries: possess them of a few inhabitants, and let those be unmolested by Indians and enemies, the land will soon swarm with inhabitants. But when a feeble band only are gathered together and obliged to contend with pestilence, famine, and the sword, their melancholy numbers will decrease and waste away. The situation of our ancestors has often been described in language that did honor to the hearts that conceived it. The boisterous ocean, with unknown shores, hemmed them in on one side; and a forest, swarming with savages yelling for their blood, threatened on the other. But the same undaunted spirit which has defended them in so many perils buoyed them above despair in their early struggles for safety and liberty. I shall be pardoned for the digression when I observe that I have in all my travels felt a degree of pride in recollecting that I belonged to a country whose valor was distinguished and whose spirit had never been debased by servile submission.

At the age of fourteen, in 1744, I made a visit from Leominster to Charlestown to visit my parents. Through a long wilderness from Lunenburg to Lower Ashuelot, now Swanzey, we travelled two days: a solitary house was all the mark of cultivation that occurred on the journey. Guided by marked trees, we travelled cautiously through the gloomy forest where now the well-tilled farms occupy each rod of ground. From Ashuelot to Charlestown the passage was opposed, now by the Hill of Difficulty, and now by the Slough Despond. A few solitary inhabitants, who appeared the representatives of wretchedness, were scattered on the way.

When I approached the town of Charlestown, the first object that met my eyes was a party of Indians holding a war dance: a cask of rum, which the inhabitants had suffered them to partake of, had raised their spirits to all the horrid yells and feats of distortion which characterize the nation. I was chilled at the sight, and passed tremblingly by. At this time Charlestown contained nine or ten families, who lived in huts not far distant from each other. The Indians were numerous, and associated in a friendly manner with the whites. It was the most northerly settlement on Connecticut River, and the adjacent country was terribly wild. A saw mill was erected, and the first boards were sawed while I was there. The inhabitants commemorated the event with a dance, which took place on the new boards. In those days there was such a mixture on the frontiers of savages and settlers, without established laws to govern them, that the state of society cannot be easily described; and the impending dangers of war, where it was known that the savages would join the enemies of our country, retarded the progress of refinement and cultivation. The inhabitants of Charlestown began to erect a fort, and took some steps towards clearing their farms; but war soon checked their industry.

Charlestown

In the year 1740 the first settlement was made in the town of Charlestown, then known by the name of No. 4, by three families, who emigrated from Lunenburg, by the name of Farnsworth: that part of New Hampshire west of Merrimack River was then a trackless wilderness. Within a few years past instances have been known of new townships, totally uninhabited, becoming flourishing and thick-settled villages in the course of six or seven years. But in those days, when government was weak, when savages were on our borders and Frenchmen in Canada, population extended with timorous and tardy paces: in the course of twelve years the families increased only to twenty-two or three. The human race will not flourish unless fostered by the warm sunshine of peace.

During the first twenty years of its existence as a settled place, until the peace between Great Britain and France, it suffered all the consternation and ravages of war; not that warfare which civilized nations wage with each other, but the cruel carnage of savages and Frenchmen. Sometimes engaged in the duties of the camp, at others sequestering themselves from surrounding enemies, they became familiar with danger, but not with industrious husbandry.

In the year 1744 the inhabitants began to erect a fort for their safety. When the Cape Breton war commenced the Indians assumed the hatchet and began their depredations on Charlestown on the 19th of April, 1746, by burning the mills and taking Captain John Spafford, Isaac Parker, and Stephen Farnsworth prisoners. On the 2d of May following Seth Putnam was killed. Two days after Captain Payne arrived with a troop of horse, from Massachusetts, to defend the place. About twenty of his men had the curiosity to view the place where Putnam was killed, and were ambushed by the Indians. Captain Stevens, who commanded a few men, rushed out of the fort to their relief: a sharp combat ensued, in which the Indians were routed. They left some guns and blankets on the field of action; but they carried their dead off with them, which is a policy they never omit. Ensign Obadiah Sartwell was captured; and Samuel Farnsworth, Elijah Allen, Peter Perin, Aaron Lyon, and Joseph Massey fell victims to Indian vengeance.

On the 19th of June a severe engagement took place. Captain Brown, from Stow, in Massachusetts, had previously arrived with some troops: a party of his joined a number of Captain Stevens's soldiers to go into the meadow after their horses. The dogs discovered an ambush, which put them into a posture for action and gave them the advantage of the first fire. This disconcerted the savages, who, being on higher ground, overshot and did but little damage to the English. The enemy were routed, and even seen to drag several dead bodies after them. They left behind them guns, spears, and blankets, which sold for forty pounds, old tenor. During the time Captain Josiah Brown assisted in defending the fort Jedediah Winchel was killed; Samuel Stanhope, Cornet Baker and David Parker were wounded. During this summer the fort was entirely blockaded, and all were obliged to take refuge within the pickets.

On the 3d of August one Philips was killed within a few feet of the fort as he accidentally stepped out: at night a soldier crept to him with a rope, and he was drawn into the fort and interred. In the summer of the year 1746 Captain Ephraim Brown, from Sudbury, arrived with a troop of horse to relieve Captain Josiah Brown. The Sudbury troop tarried about a month, and were relieved by a company commanded by Captain Winchester, who defended the place till autumn, when the inhabitants, fatigued with watching and weary of the dangers of the forest, deserted the place entirely for about six months. In the month of August, previous to the evacuation, the Indians, assisted by their brethren the French, were very troublesome and mischievous: they destroyed all the horses, hogs, and cattle. An attack was made on the fort which lasted two days. My father at this time lost ten cattle; but the people were secured behind their wooden walls, and received but little damage.

In this recess of the settlement of No. 4 the Indians and French were icelocked in Canada, and the frontiers suffered only in apprehension. In March, 1747, Captain Phinehas Stevens, who commanded a ranging party of about thirty men, marched to No. 4 and took possession of the fort. He found it uninjured by the enemy; and an old spaniel and a cat, who had been domesticated before the evacuation, had guarded it safely through the winter, and gave the troops a hearty welcome to their tenement.

Captain Stevens was of eminent service to the infant settlement. In 1748 he moved his family to the place, and encouraged the settlers by his fortitude and industry. In the early part of his life, when Rutland suffered by savage vengeance, when the Rev. Mr. Willard was murdered, he was taken prisoner and carried to St. Francis. This informed him of the Indian customs and familiarized him with their mode of warfare. He was an active, penetrating soldier, and a respectable, worthy citizen.

In a few days after the fort was taken possession of by Captain Stevens's troops a party of five hundred French and Indians, commanded by Monsieur Debelcie, sallied from their den in Canada and made a furious attack on the fort. The battle lasted five days, and every stratagem which French policy or Indian malice could invent was practised to reduce the garrison. Sometimes they made an onset by a discharge of musketry; at others they discharged fire arrows, which communicated fire to several parts of the fort. But these were insufficient to daunt the courage of the little band that were assailed. Their next step was to fill a cart with combustibles, and roll it against the walls, to communicate fire; but the English kept up such a brisk, incessant fire that they were defeated in the project. At length the monsieurs, tired with fighting, beat a parley. Two Indians, formerly acquainted with Captain Stevens, came as negotiators, and wished to exchange some furs for corn: this Captain Stevens refused, but offered a bushel of corn for each hostage they would leave to be exchanged at some future day. These terms were not complied with; and on the fifth day the enemy retreated, at which time the soldiers in the garrison honored them with as brisk a discharge as they could afford, to let them know that they were neither disheartened nor exhausted in ammunition. The garrison had none killed; and only one, by the name of Brown, was wounded.

Perhaps no place was ever defended with greater bravery than this fort during this action. Thirty or forty men, when attacked by five hundred, must have an uncommon degree of fortitude and vigilance to defend themselves during a siege of five days. But Captain Stevens was equal to the task, and will be applauded by posterity. After the battle he sent an express to Boston with the tidings. Governor Charles Knowles happened then to be at Boston, and rewarded Captain Stevens with a handsome sword; in gratitude for which the place was afterwards called Charlestown.

In November, 1747, a body of the troops set out from the fort to return to Massachusetts. They had not proceeded far before the Indians fired on them. Isaac Goodale and Nathaniel Gould were killed, and one Anderson taken prisoner. From this period until the end of the Cape Breton war the fort was defended by Captain Stevens. Soldiers passed and repassed to Canada; but the inhabitants took sanctuary in the fort, and made but little progress in cultivation. During the Indian wars, which lasted till the year 1760, Charlestown was noted more for its feats of war than a place of rapid improvement. Settlers thought it more prudent to remain with their friends in safety than risk their scalps with savage power. Since that period it has become a flourishing village, and contains all that a rural situation affords of the useful and the pleasant. Numerous farms and stately buildings now flourish where the savage roamed the forest. The prosperity of the town was greatly promoted by the Rev. Bulkely Olcott, who was a settled minister there about thirty-two years. In the character of this good man were combined the agreeable companion, the industrious citizen, and the unaffected Christian. During the whole of his ministry his solicitude for the happiness of his parishioners was as conspicuous in the benefits they received from his assistance as in their sincere attachment to his person. As a divine he was pathetic, devout, and instructive, and may with propriety be said to have

Shown the path to heaven, and led the way.

He was highly respected through life. In June, 1793, he died, much lamented.

Removal to Charlestown, &c.

In May, 1749, we received information of the cessation of arms between Great Britain and France. I had then been married about two years, and Mr. Johnson's enterprising spirit was zealous to remove to Charlestown. In June we undertook the hazardous and fatiguing journey. We arrived safe at the fort, and found five families, who had ventured so far into the woods during hostilities. But the gloomy forest and the warlike appearance of the place soon made me homesick. Two or three days after my arrival orders came from Massachusetts to withdraw the troops. Government placed confidence in the proffered peace of Frenchmen, and withdrew even the appearance of hostility. But French treachery and savage malice will ever keep pace with each other. Without even the suspicion of danger, the inhabitants went about their business of husbandry. The day the soldiers left the fort Ensign Obadiah Sartwell went to harrow some corn, and took Enos Stevens, the fourth son of Phinehas Stevens, Esq., to ride horse: my father and two brothers were at work in the meadow. Early in the afternoon the Indians appeared and shot Ensign Sartwell and the horse, and took young Stevens a prisoner. In addition to this my father and brothers were in the meadow, and we supposed they must be destroyed. My husband was gone to Northfield. In the fort were seven women and four men: the anxiety and grief we experienced were the highest imaginable. The next night we despatched a post to Boston to carry the news of our disaster; but my father and brothers did not return. The next day but one my husband and five or six others arrived from Northfield. We kept close in the garrison, suffering every apprehension for ten or twelve days, when the sentry from the box cried out that troops were coming: joyful at the relief, we all mounted on the top of the fort, and among the rest discovered my father. He, on hearing the guns, supposed the fort was destroyed, left his team in the meadow, and made the best of his way to Northfield with my two brothers. The soldiers were about thirty in number, and headed by Major Josiah Willard, of Fort Dummer. Enos Stevens was carried to Montreal; but the French commander sent him back directly by the way of Albany. This was the last damage done the frontiers during the Cape Breton war.

Cursory Notices

A detail of the miseries of a "frontier man" must excite the pity of every child of humanity. The gloominess of the rude forest, the distance from friends and competent defence, and the daily inroads and nocturnal yells of hostile Indians, awaken those keen apprehensions and anxieties which conception only can picture. If the peaceful employment of husbandry is pursued, the loaded musket must stand by his side; if he visits a neighbor, or resorts on Sundays to the sacred house of prayer, the weapons of war must bear him company; at home the distresses of a wife and the tears of lisping children often unman the soul that real danger assailed in vain. Those who can recollect the war that existed between France and England fifty years ago may figure to themselves the unhappy situation of the inhabitants on the frontiers of New Hampshire: the malice of the French in Canada, and the exasperated savages that dwelt in their vicinity, rendered the tedious days and frightful nights a season of unequalled calamities. The daily reports of captured families and slaughtered friends mingled grief with fear. Had there been an organized government to stretch forth its protecting arm in any case of danger, the misery might have been in a degree alleviated. But the infancy of our country did not admit of this blessing. While Governor Shirley, of Massachusetts, was petitioning to England for a fleet and an army, Benning Wentworth, the supine governor of New Hampshire, obeyed implicitly the advice of his friend Shirley, and remained inactively secure at his seat at Portsmouth. At the commencement of the year 1745 the Quixotic expedition to Louisburg was projected, the success of which originated from the merest accident rather than from military valor or generalship: this drained the thinly inhabited State of New Hampshire of most of its effective men. From that period till the peace, which took place in the year 1749, the visionary schemes of Shirley kept the best soldiers imbodied in some remote place, as a force to execute some impolitic project. The conquest of Canada and the attack upon Crown Point are recorded as specimens of the wild projects which were to employ the infant forces of New England. During this time the frontiers sustained additional miseries by having the small forces of the state deducted for purposes which could be of no immediate service to them. The savages committed frequent depredations on the defenceless inhabitants; and the ease with which they gained their prey encouraged their boldness, and by scattering in small parties they were able to infest the whole frontier of New Hampshire, from Fort Dummer, on Connecticut

River, to the lowest settlement on the Merrimack. During this war, which is known by the name of the Cape Breton war, the town of No. 4 could hardly be said to be inhabited: some adventurers had made a beginning, but few were considered as belonging to the town. Captain Stevens, whose valor is recorded as an instance of consummate generalship, part of the time kept the fort, which afforded a shelter to the enterprising settlers in times of imminent danger. But even his vigilance did not save the town from numerous scenes of carnage. At the commencement of the peace, in 1749, the enterprising spirit of New England rose superior to the dangers of the forest, and they began to venture innovation. The Indians, still thirsty for plunder and rapine, and regardless of the peace which their masters the French had concluded, kept up a flying warfare, and committed several outrages upon lives and property. This kept the increasing inhabitants in a state of alarm for three or four years: most of the time they performed their daily work without molestation, but retreated to the fort at each returning night.

Our country has so long been exposed to Indian wars that recitals of exploits and sufferings, of escapes and deliverances, have become both numerous and trite. The air of novelty will not be attempted in the following pages: simple facts, unadorned, are what the reader must expect: pity for my sufferings and admiration at my safe return is all that my history can excite. The aged man, while perusing, will probably turn his attention to the period when the facts took place; his memory will be refreshed with the sad tidings of his country's sufferings, which gave a daily wound to his feelings, between the years 1740 and 1760. By contrasting those days with the present he may rejoice that he witnesses those times which many have "waited for, but died without the sight." Those "in early life," while they commiserate the sufferings which their parents and ancestors endured, may felicitate themselves that their lines fell in a land of peace, where neither savages nor neighboring wars molest their happiness.

Situation until August 31, 1754

Some of the soldiers who arrived with Major Willard, with the inhabitants who bore arms, were commanded by Captain Stevens the rest of the year 1749 and part of the following spring; after which the inhabitants resided pretty much in the fort until the spring or fall of the year 1752. They cultivated their lands in some degree, but they put but little confidence in the savages.

The continuation of peace began by degrees to appease the resentment of the Indians, and they appeared to discover a wish for friendly intercourse. The inhabitants in No. 4 and its vicinity relaxed their watchfulness and ventured more boldly into their fields. Every appearance of hostility at length vanished. The Indians expressed a wish to traffic; the inhabitants laid by their fears, and thought no more of tomahawks or scalping knives. Mr. Johnson now thought himself justified in removing to his farm, a hundred rods distant from the fort, which was then the uppermost settlement on Connecticut River. He pursued his occupation of trade, and the Indians made frequent visits to traffic their furs for his merchandise. He frequently credited them for blankets and other necessaries, and in most instances they were punctual in payment. During the year 1753 all was harmony and safety; settlements increased with tolerable rapidity; and the new country began to assume the appearance of cultivation.

The commencement of the year 1754 began to threaten another rupture between the French and English; and as the dividing line between Canada and the English colonies was the object of contention, it was readily seen that the frontier towns would be in imminent danger. But as immediate war was not expected, Mr. Johnson thought that he might risk the safety of his family while he made a tour to Connecticut for trade. He set out the last of May; and his absence of three months was a tedious and a bitter season to me. Soon after his departure every body was "tremblingly alive" with fear. The Indians were reported to be on their march for our destruction; and our distance from sources of information gave full latitude for exaggeration of news before it reached our ears. The fears of the night were horrible beyond description; and even the light of day was far from dispelling painful anxiety. While looking from the windows of my log house and seeing my neighbors tread cautiously by each hedge and hillock lest some secreted savage might start forth to take their scalp, my fears would baffle description. Alarms grew louder and louder, till our apprehensions were too strongly confirmed by the news of the capture of Mr. Malloon's family on Merrimack River. This reached us about the 20th of August. Imagination now saw and heard a thousand Indians; and I never went round my own house without first looking with trembling caution by each corner to see if a tomahawk was not raised for my destruction.

On the 24th of August I was relieved from all my fears by the arrival of my husband. He brought intelligence from Connecticut that a war was expected the next spring, but that no immediate danger was contemplated. He had made preparations to remove to Northfield as soon as our stock of hay was consumed and our dozen of swine had demolished our ample stores of grain, which would secure his family and property from the miseries and ravages of war. Our eldest son, Sylvanus, who was six years old, was in the mean time to be put to school at Springfield. Mr. Johnson brought home a large addition to his stores, and the neighbors made frequent parties at our house to express their joy for his return; and time passed merrily off by the aid of spirit and a ripe yard of melons. As I was in the last days of pregnancy, I could not join so heartily in their good cheer as I otherwise might. Yet in a new country pleasure is often derived from sources unknown to those less accustomed to the woods. The return of my husband, the relief from danger, and the crowds of happy friends combined to render my situation peculiarly agreeable. I now boasted with exultation that I should, with husband, friends, and luxuries, live happy in spite of the fear of savages.

On the evening of the 29th of August our house was visited by a party of neighbors, who spent the time very cheerfully with watermelons and flip till midnight. They all then retired in high spirits except a spruce young spark, who tarried to keep company with my sister. We then went to bed with feelings well tuned for sleep, and rested with fine composure till midway between daybreak and sunrise, when we were roused by neighbor Labarree's knocking at the door, who had shouldered his axe to do a day's work for my husband. Mr. Johnson slipped on his jacket and trousers and stepped to the door to let him in. But by opening the door he opened a scene terrible to describe. "Indians! Indians!" were the first words I heard. He sprang to his guns; but Labarree, heedless of danger, instead of closing the door to keep them out, began to rally our hired men up stairs for not rising earlier. But in an instant a crowd of savages, fixed horribly for war, rushed furiously in. I screamed and begged my friends to ask for quarter. By this time they were all over the house—some up stairs, some hauling my sister out of bed; another had hold of me; and one was approaching Mr. Johnson, who stood in the middle of the floor to deliver himself up. But the Indian, supposing that he would make resistance and be more than his match, went to the door and brought three of his comrades, and the four bound him. I was led to the door, fainting and trembling. There stood my friend Labarree bound. Ebenezer Farnsworth, whom they found up chamber, they were putting in the same situation; and, to complete the shocking scene, my three little children were driven naked to the place where I stood. On viewing myself I found that I, too, was naked. An Indian had plundered three gowns, who, on seeing my situation, gave me the whole. I asked another for a petticoat; but he refused it. After what little plunder their hurry would allow them to get was confusedly bundled up, we were ordered to march. After going about twenty rods we fell behind a rising ground, where we halted to pack the things in a better manner: while there a savage went back, as we supposed, to fire the buildings. Farnsworth proposed to my husband to go back with him, to get a quantity of pork from the cellar to help us on our journey; but Mr. Johnson prudently replied, that, by that means, the Indians might find the rum, and in a fit of intoxication kill us all. The Indian presently returned with marks of fear in his countenance, and we were hurried on with all violence. Two savages laid hold of each of my arms, and hurried me through thorny thickets in a most unmerciful manner. I lost a shoe and suffered exceedingly. We heard the alarm guns from the fort. This added new speed to the flight of the savages. They were apprehensive that soldiers might be sent for our relief. When we had got a mile and a half my faintness obliged me to sit. This being observed by an Indian, he drew his knife, as I supposed, to put an end to my existence. But he only cut some band with which my gown was tied, and then pushed me on. My little children were crying, my husband and the other two men were bound, and my sister and myself were obliged to make the best of our way with all our might. The loss of my shoe rendered travelling extremely painful. At the distance of three miles there was a general halt. The savages, supposing that we as well as themselves might have an appetite for breakfast, gave us a loaf of bread, some raisins, and apples which they had taken from the house. While we were forcing down our scanty breakfast a horse came in sight, known to us all by the name of Scoggin, belonging to Phinehas Stevens, Esq. One of the Indians attempted to shoot him, but was prevented by Mr. Johnson. They then expressed a wish to catch him, saying, by pointing to me, for squaw to ride. My husband had previously been unbound to assist the children; he, with two Indians, caught the horse on the banks of the river. By this time my legs and feet were covered with blood, which being noticed by Mr. Labarree, he, with that humanity which never forsook him, took his own stockings and presented them to me, and the Indians gave me a pair of moccasons. Bags and blankets were thrown over Scoggin, and I mounted on the top of them, and on we jogged about seven miles to the upper end of Wilcott's Island. We there halted and prepared to cross the river. Rafts were made of dry timber. Two Indians and Farnsworth crossed first; Labarree, by signs, got permission to swim the horse; and Mr. Johnson was allowed to swim by the raft that I was on, to push it along. We all arrived safe on the other side of the river about four o'clock in the afternoon. A fire was kindled, and some of their stolen kettles

were hung over it and filled with porridge. The savages took delight in
viewing their spoil, which amounted to forty or fifty pounds in value.
They then with a true savage yell gave the war whoop and bade defiance
to danger. As our tarry in this place lasted an hour, I had time to reflect
on our miserable situation. Captives, in the power of unmerciful savages,
without provision and almost without clothes, in a wilderness where we
must sojourn as long as the children of Israel did for aught we knew;
and, what added to our distress, not one of our savage masters could
understand a word of English. Here, after being hurried from home with
such rapidity, I have leisure to inform the reader respecting our Indian
masters. They were eleven in number, men of middle age except one, a
youth of sixteen, who in our journey discovered a very mischievous and
troublesome disposition. According to their national practice, he who
first laid hands on a prisoner considered him as his property. My master,
who was the one that took my hand when I sat on the bed, was as clever
an Indian as ever I saw. He even evinced, at numerous times, a disposition that showed he was by no means void of compassion. The four
who took my husband claimed him as their property; and my sister,
three children, Labarree, and Farnsworth had each a master. When the
time came for us to prepare to march I almost expired at the thought of
leaving my aged parents, brothers, sisters, and friends, and travel with
savages through a dismal forest to unknown regions, in the alarming
situation I then was in, with three small children. The eldest, Sylvanus,
was but six years old; my eldest daughter, Susanna, was four; and Polly,
the other, two. My sister Miriam was fourteen. My husband was barefoot, and otherwise thinly clothed. His master had taken his jacket, and
nothing but his shirt and trousers remained. My two daughters had
nothing but their shifts, and I only the gown that was handed me by the
savages. In addition to the sufferings which arose from my own deplorable condition, I could not but feel for my friend Labarree. He had
left a wife and four small children behind to lament his loss and to render
his situation extremely unhappy. With all these misfortunes lying heavily
upon me, the reader can imagine my situation. The Indians pronounced
the dreadful word "munch," march; and on we must go. I was put on
the horse; Mr. Johnson took one daughter; and Mr. Labarree, being
unbound, took the other. We went six or eight miles and stopped for
the night. The men were made secure by having their legs put in split
sticks, somewhat like stocks, and tied with cords, which were tied to
the limbs of trees too high to be reached. My sister, much to her mortification, must lie between two Indians, with a cord thrown over her
and passing under each of them. The little children had blankets; and I

was allowed one for my use. Thus we took lodging for the night, with the sky for a covering and the ground for a pillow. The fatigues of the preceding day obliged me to sleep several hours, in spite of the horrors which surrounded me. The Indians observed great silence, and never spoke but when really necessary; and all the prisoners were disposed to say but little. My children were much more peaceable than could be imagined; gloomy fear imposed a deadly silence.

History of our Journey through the Wilderness till we came to the Waters that enter Lake Champlain

In the morning we were roused before sunrise: the Indians struck up a fire, hung on their stolen kettles, and made us some water gruel for breakfast. After a few sips of this meagre fare I was again put on the horse, with my husband by my side to hold me on. My two fellow-prisoners took the little girls, and we marched sorrowfully on for an hour or two, when a keener distress was added to my multiplied afflictions. I was taken with the pangs of childbirth. The Indians signified to us that we must go on to a brook. When we got there they showed some humanity by making a booth for me. Here the compassionate reader will drop a fresh tear for my inexpressible distress; fifteen or twenty miles from the abode of any civilized being, in the open wilderness, rendered cold by a rainy day, in one of the most perilous hours, and unsupplied with the least necessary that could yield convenience in the hazardous moment. My children were crying at a distance, where they were held by their masters, and only my husband and sister to attend me. None but mothers can figure to themselves my unhappy fortune. The Indians kept aloof the whole time. About ten o'clock a daughter was born. They then brought me some articles of clothing for the child which they had taken from the house. My master looked into the booth and clapped his hands with joy, crying, "Two moneys for me! two moneys for me!" I was permitted to rest the remainder of the day. The Indians were employed in making a bier for the prisoners to carry me on, and another booth for my lodging during night. They brought a needle, and two pins, and some bark to tie the child's clothes, which they gave my sister, and a large wooden spoon to feed it with. At dusk they made some porridge, and brought a cup to steep some roots in, which Mr. Labarree had provided. In the evening I was removed to the new booth. For supper they made more porridge and some johnny cakes. My portion was brought me in a little bark. I slept that night far beyond expectation.

In the morning we were summoned for the journey, after the usual breakfast of meal and water. I, with my infant in my arms, was laid on the litter, which was supported alternately by Mr. Johnson, Labarree, and Farnsworth. My sister and son were put upon Scoggin, and the two little girls rode on their masters' backs. Thus we proceeded two miles, when my carriers grew too faint to proceed any farther. This being observed by our sable masters, a general halt was called, and they imbodied themselves for council. My master soon made signs to Mr. Johnson that if I could ride on the horse I might proceed, otherwise I must be left behind. Here I observed marks of pity in his countenance; but this might arise from the fear of losing his two moneys. I preferred an attempt to ride on the horse rather than to perish miserably alone. Mr. Labarree took the infant, and every step of the horse almost deprived me of life. My weak and helpless condition rendered me, in a degree, insensible to every thing. My poor child could have no sustenance from my breast, and was supported entirely by water gruel. My other little children, rendered peevish by an uneasy mode of riding, often burst into cries; but a surly check from their masters soon silenced them. We proceeded on with a slow, mournful pace. My weakness was too severe to allow me to sit on the horse long at a time. Every hour I was taken off and laid on the ground to rest. This preserved my life during the third day. At night we found ourselves at the head of Black River Pond. Here we prepared to spend the night. Our supper consisted of gruel and the broth of a hawk they had killed the preceding day. The prisoners were secured as usual, a booth was made for me, and all went to rest. After encampment we entered into a short conversation. My sister observed, that, if I could have been left behind, our trouble would have been seemingly nothing. My husband hoped, by the assistance of Providence, we should all be preserved. Mr. Labarree pitied his poor family; and Farnsworth summed the whole of his wishes by saying, that, if he could have got a layer of pork from the cellar, we should not be in fear of starvation. The night was uncommonly dark, and passed tediously off.

In the morning, half chilled with a cold fog, we were ordered from our places of rest, were offered the lean fare of meal and water, and then prepared for the journey. Every thing resembled a funeral procession. The savages preserved their gloomy sadness. The prisoners, bowed down with grief and fatigue, felt little disposition to talk; and the unevenness of the country, sometimes lying in miry plains, at others rising into steep and broken hills, rendered our passage hazardous and painful. Mr. Labarree kept the infant in his arms and preserved its life. The fifth day's journey was an unvaried scene of fatigue. The Indians sent out two or three hunting parties, who returned without game. As we had in the morning consumed the last morsel of our meal, every one now began to be seriously alarmed; and hunger, with all its horrors, looked us earnestly in the face. At night we found the waters that run into Lake Champlain, which was over the height of land. Before dark we halted; and the Indians, by the help of their punk, which they carried in horns, made a fire. They soon adopted a plan to relieve their hunger. The horse was shot, and his flesh was in a few moments broiling on embers; and they, with native gluttony, satiated their craving appetites. To use the term politeness, in the management of this repast, may be thought a burlesque; yet their offering the prisoners the best parts of the horse certainly bordered on civility. An epicure could not have catered nicer slices, nor in that situation served them up with more neatness. Appetite is said to be the best sauce; yet our abundance of it did not render savory this novel steak. My children, however, ate too much, which made them very unwell for a number of days. Broth was made for me and my child, which was rendered almost a luxury by the seasoning of roots. After supper countenances began to brighten. Those who had relished the meal exhibited new strength, and those who had only snuffed its effluvia confessed themselves regaled. The evening was employed in drying and smoking what remained for future use. The night was a scene of distressing fears to me; and my extreme weakness had affected my mind to such a degree that every difficulty appeared doubly terrible. By the assistance of Scoggin I had been brought so far; yet so great was my debility that every hour I was taken off and laid on the ground, to keep me from expiring. But now, alas! this conveyance was no more. To walk was impossible. Inevitable death, in the midst of woods one hundred miles wide, appeared my only portion.

Our Arrival at East Bay, in Lake Champlain

In the morning of the sixth day the Indians exerted themselves to prepare one of their greatest dainties. The marrow bones of old Scoggin were pounded for a soup; and every root, both sweet and bitter, that the woods afforded, was thrown in to give it a flavor. Each one partook of as much as his feelings would allow. The war whoop then resounded, with an infernal yell, and we began to fix for a march. My fate was unknown, till my master brought some bark and tied my petticoats as high as he supposed would be convenient for walking, and ordered me to "munch." With scarce strength to stand alone, I went on half a mile with my little son and three Indians. The rest were advanced. My power to move then failed; the world grew dark, and I dropped down. I had sight enough to see an Indian lift his hatchet over my head; while my little son screamed, "Ma'am, do go; for they will kill you." As I fainted, my last thought was, that I should presently be in the world of spirits. When I awoke my master was talking angrily with the savage who had threatened my life. By his gestures I could learn that he charged him with not acting the honorable part of a warrior, by an attempt to destroy the prize of a brother. A whoop was given for a halt. My master helped me to the rest of the company, where a council was held, the result of which was, that my husband should walk by my side and help me along. This he did for some hours; but faintness then overpowered me, and Mr. Johnson's tenderness and solicitude were unequal to the task of aiding me farther. Another council was held: while in debate, as I lay on the ground gasping for breath, my master sprang towards me with his hatchet. My husband and fellow-prisoners grew pale at the sight, suspecting that he by a single blow would rid themselves of so great a burden as myself. But he had yet too much esteem for his "two moneys." His object was to get bark from a tree, to make a pack saddle for my conveyance on the back of my husband. He took me up, and we marched in that form the rest of the day. Mr. Labarree still kept my infant. Farnsworth carried one of the little girls, and the other rode with her master. They were extremely sick and weak, owing to the large portion of the horse which they ate; but if they uttered a murmuring word, a menacing frown from the savages soon imposed silence. None of the Indians were disposed to show insults of any nature except the youngest, which I have before mentioned. He often delighted himself by tormenting my sister, by pulling her hair, treading on her gown, and numerous other boyish pranks, which were provoking and troublesome. We moved on, faint and wearily, till night. The Indians then yelled their war whoop, built a fire, and hung over their horse broth. After supper my booth was built as usual, and I reposed much better than I had the preceding nights.

In the morning I found myself greatly restored. Without the aid of physicians, or physic, Nature had begun the cure of that weakness to which she had reduced me but a few days before. The reader will be tired of the repetition of the same materials for our meals; but if my feelings can be realized, no one will turn with disgust from a breakfast of steaks which were cut from the thigh of a horse. After which Mr. Johnson was ordered to take the infant and go forward with part of the company. I "munched" in the rear till we came to a beaver pond, which was formed in a branch of Otter Creek. Here I was obliged to wade.

When half way over, up to the middle in cold water, my little strength failed, and my power to speak or see left me. While motionless and stiffened, in the middle of the pond, I was perceived from the other side by Mr. Johnson, who laid down the infant and came to my assistance. He took me in his arms; and when the opposite side was gained, life itself had apparently forsaken me. The whole company stopped; and the Indians, with more humanity than I supposed them possessed of, busied themselves in making a fire to warm me into life. The warm influence of the fire restored my exhausted strength by degrees; and in two hours I was told to munch. The rest of the day I was carried by my husband. In the middle of the afternoon we arrived on the banks of one of the great branches of Otter Creek. Here we halted; and two savages, who had been on a hunting scout, returned with a duck. A fire was made, which was thrice grateful to my cold, shivering limbs. Six days had now almost elapsed since the fatal morn in which we were taken; and by the blessing of that Providence whose smiles give life to creation we were still in existence. My wearied husband, naked children, and helpless infant formed a scene that conveyed severer pangs to my heart than all the sufferings I endured myself. The Indians were sullen and silent; the prisoners were swollen with gloomy grief; and I was half the time expiring. After my feelings were a little quickened by warmth, my sad portion was brought in a bark, consisting of the duck's head and a gill of broth. As I lifted the unsavory morsel with a trembling hand to my mouth, I cast my thoughts back a few days to a time when, from a board plentifully spread in my own house, I ate my food with a merry heart. The wooden spoon dropped from my feeble hand. The contrast was too affecting. Seated on a ragged rock, beneath a hemlock, as I then was, emaciated by sickness, and surrounded by my weeping and distressed family, who were helpless prisoners, despair would have robbed me of life, had I not put my whole confidence in that Being who has power to save. Our masters began to prepare to ford the stream. I swallowed most of my broth, and was taken up by my husband. The river was very rapid and passing dangerous. Mr. Labarree, when half over with my child, was tripped up by its rapidity, and lost the babe in the water: little did I expect to see the poor thing again; but he fortunately reached a corner of its blanket and saved its life. The rest got safe to the other shore; another fire was built, and my sister dried the infant and its clothes.

Here the savages for the first time gave loud tokens of joy, by hallooing and yelling in a tremendous manner. The prisoners were now introduced to a new school. Little did we expect that the accomplishment of dancing would ever be taught us by the savages. But the war dance must now be held, and every prisoner that could move must take its awkward steps. The figure consisted of circular motion round the fire; each sang his own music, and the best dancer was the one most violent in motion. The prisoners were taught each a song; mine was, *Danna witchee natche-pung;* my son's was, *Narwiscumpton.* The rest I cannot recollect. Whether this task was imposed on us for their diversion, or a religious ceremonial, I cannot say; but it was very painful and offensive. In the forenoon seven Indians came to us, who were received with great joy by our masters, who took great pleasure in introducing their prisoners. The war dance was again held; we were obliged to join and sing our songs, while the Indians rent the air with infernal yelling. We then embarked, and arrived at Crown Point about noon. Each prisoner was then led by his master to the residence of the French commander. The Indians kept up their infernal yelling the whole time. We were ordered to his apartment, and used with that hospitality which characterizes the best part of the nation. We had brandy in profusion, a good dinner, and a change of linen. This was luxury indeed, after what we had suffered for the want of these things. None but ourselves could prize their value. We, after dinner, were paraded before Mr. Commander and underwent examination; after which we were shown a convenient apartment, where we resided four days, not subject to the jurisdiction of our savage masters. Here we received great civilities and many presents. I had a nurse, who in a great measure restored my exhausted strength. My children were all decently clothed, and my infant in particular. The first day, while I was taking a nap, they dressed it so fantastically, *à la France,* that I refused to own it when brought to my bedside, not guessing that I was the mother of such a strange thing.

On the fourth day, to our great grief and mortification, we were again delivered to the Indians, who led us to the water side, where we all embarked in one vessel for St. John's. The wind shifted after a short sail, and we dropped anchor. In a little time a canoe came alongside of us, in which was a white woman, who was bound for Albany. Mr. Johnson begged her to stop a few minutes while he wrote to Colonel Lydius, of Albany, to inform him of our situation, and to request him to put the same in the Boston newspapers, that our friends might learn that we were alive. The woman delivered the letter, and the contents were published, which conveyed the agreeable tidings to our friends, that, although prisoners, we were then alive.

The following letter, in return for the one we sent to Colonel Lydius, was the first we received from New England:—

ALBANY, November 5, 1754

SIR,—I received yours of the 5th of October, with a letter or two for New England, which I have forwarded immediately, and have wrote to Boston, in which I urged the government to endeavor your and family's redemption as soon as conveniency would admit.

I am quite sorry for your doleful misfortune, and hope the just God will endue you with patience to undergo your troubles, and justly use his rewards on the evil doers and authors of your misfortune. Present my service to all the prisoners with you, from him who subscribes himself to be

Your very humble servant,

JOHN W. LYDIUS

Lieutenant James Johnson, Montreal

After a disagreeable voyage of three days, we made St. John's the 16th of September, where we again experienced the politeness of a French commander. I, with my child, was kindly lodged in the same room with himself and lady. In the morning we still found misfortune treading close at our heels: we must again be delivered to our savage masters, and take another passage in the boats for Chamblee; when within three miles of which, Labarree, myself and child, with our two masters, were put on shore. We were ignorant of our destiny; and parting from my husband and friends was a severe trial, without knowing whether we were ever to meet them again. We walked on to Chamblee; here our fears were dissipated by meeting our friends. In the garrison of this place we found all the hospitality our necessities required. Here for the first, after my captivity, I lodged on a bed. Brandy was handed about in large bowls, and we lived in high style. The next morning we were put in the custody of our old masters, who took us to the canoes, in which we had a painful voyage that day and the following night to Sorell, where we arrived on the 19th. A hospitable friar came to the shore to see us, and invited us to his house. He gave us a good breakfast, and drank our better healths in a tumbler of brandy. He took compassionate notice of my child, and ordered it some suitable food. But the Indians hurried us off before it could eat. He then went with us to the shore, and ordered his servant to carry the food, prepared for the child, to the canoe, where he waited till I fed it. The friar was a very genteel man, and gave us his benediction at parting in feeling language. We then rowed on till the middle of the afternoon, when we landed on a barren heath, and by the help of a fire cooked an Indian dinner; after which the war dance was held and another infernal yelling. The prisoners were obliged to sing till they were hoarse, and dance round the fire.

We had now arrived within a few miles of the village of St. Francis, to which place our masters belonged. Whenever the warriors return from an excursion against an enemy, their return to the tribe or village must be designated by warlike ceremonial; the captives or spoil, which may happen to crown their valor, must be conducted in a triumphant form, and decorated to every possible advantage. For this end we must now submit to painting: their vermilion, with which they were ever supplied, was mixed with bear's grease, and every cheek, chin, and forehead must have a dash. We then rowed on within a mile of the town, where we stopped at a French house to dine: the prisoners were served with soup meagre and bread. After dinner two savages proceeded to the village to carry the glad tidings of our arrival. The whole atmosphere soon resounded from every quarter with whoops, yells, shrieks, and screams. St. Francis, from the noise that came from it, might be supposed the centre of pandemonium. Our masters were not backward; they made every response they possibly could. The whole time we were sailing from the French house the noise was direful to be heard. Two hours before sunset we came to the landing at the village. No sooner had we landed than the yelling in the town was redoubled; a cloud of savages, of all sizes and sexes, soon appeared running towards us. When they reached the boats they formed themselves into a long parade, leaving a small space through which we must pass. Each Indian then took his prisoner by his hand, and, after ordering him to sing the war song, began to march through the gauntlet. We expected a severe beating before we got through; but were agreeably disappointed when we found that each Indian only gave us a tap on the shoulder. We were led directly to the houses, each taking his prisoner to his own wigwam. When I entered my master's door his brother saluted me with a large belt of wampum, and my master presented me with another. Both were put over my shoulders, and crossed behind and before. My new home was not the most agreeable: a large wigwam, without a floor, with a fire in the centre, and only a few water vessels and dishes to eat from, made of birch bark, and tools for cookery, made clumsily of wood, for furniture, will not be thought a pleasing residence to one accustomed to civilized life.

Residence at St. Francis.—Sale of most of the Prisoners to the French, and Removal to Montreal

Night presently came after our arrival at St. Francis. Those who have felt the gloomy, homesick feelings which sadden those hours which a youth passes when first from a father's house, may judge of part of my sufferings; but when the rest of my circumstances are added, their conception must fall infinitely short. I now found myself, with my infant, in a large wigwam, accompanied with two or three warriors and as many squaws, where I must spend the night, and perhaps a year. My fellow-prisoners were dispersed over the town, each one, probably, feeling the same gloominess with myself. Hasty pudding presently was brought forward for supper. A spacious bowl of wood, well filled, was placed in a central spot, and each one drew near with a wooden spoon. As the Indians never use seats, nor have any in their wigwams, my awkwardness in taking my position was a matter of no small amusement to my new companions. The squaws first fall upon their knees, and then sit back upon their heels. This was a posture that I could not imitate. To sit in any other was thought by them indelicate and unpolite. But I advanced to my pudding with the best grace I could; not, however, escaping some of their funny remarks. When the hour for sleep came on, for it would be improper to call it bedtime where beds were not, I was pointed to a platform, raised half a yard, where upon a board covered with a blanket I was to pass the night. The Indians threw themselves down in various parts of the building in a manner that more resembled cows in a shed than human beings in a house. In the morning our breakfast consisted of the relics of the last night. My sister came to see me in the forenoon; and we spent some hours in observations upon our situation while washing some apparel at a little brook. In the afternoon I, with my infant, was taken to the grand parade, where we found a large collection of the village inhabitants. An aged chief stepped forward into an area, and after every noise was silenced and every one fixed in profound attention he began to harangue: his manner was solemn; his motions and expression gave me a perfect idea of an orator. Not a breath was heard, and every spectator seemed to reverence what he said. After the speech my little son was brought to the opposite side of the parade, and a number of blankets laid by his side. It now appeared that his master and mine intended an exchange of prisoners. My master, being a hunter, wished for my son to attend him on his excursions. Each delivered his property with great formality; my son and blankets being an equivalent for myself, child, and wampum. I was taken to the house of my new master, and found myself allied to the first family. My master, whose name was Gill, was son-in-law to the grand sachem, was accounted rich, had a store of goods, and lived in a style far above the majority of his tribe. He often told me that he had an English heart, but his wife was true Indian blood. Soon after my arrival at his house the interpreter came to inform me that I was adopted into his family. I was then introduced into the family, and was told to call them brothers and sisters. I made a short reply, expressive of gratitude for being introduced to a house of high rank, and requested their patience while I should learn the customs of the nation. This was scarce over when the attention of the village was called to the grand parade, to attend a rejoicing occasioned by the arrival of some warriors who had brought some scalps. They were carried in triumph on a pole. Savage butchery upon murdered countrymen! The sight was horrid. As I retired to my new residence I could hear the savage yells that accompanied the war dance. I spent the night in sad reflection.

My time now was solitary beyond description. My new sisters and brothers treated me with the same attention that they did their natural kindred; but it was an unnatural situation to me. I was a novice at making canoes, bunks, and tumplines, which was the only occupation of the squaws; of course, idleness was among my calamities. My fellow-prisoners were as gloomy as myself; ignorant whether they were to spend their days in this inactive village, to be carried into a war campaign, to slaughter their countrymen, or to be dragged to the cold lakes of the north in a hunting voyage. We visited each other daily, and spent our time in conjecturing our future destiny.

The space of forty-two years having elapsed since my residence in St. Francis, it is impossible to give the reader a minute detail of events that occurred while there: many of them are still forcibly impressed upon my memory; but dates and particulars are now inaccurately treasured up by faint recollection. Mr. Johnson tarried but a few days with me before he was carried to Montreal to be sold. My two daughters, sister, and Labarree were soon after carried to the same place at different times. Farnsworth was carried by his master on a hunting scout; but not proving so active in the chase and ambush as they wished, he was returned and sent to Montreal. I now found an increase to my trouble: with only my son and infant in this strange land, without a prospect of relief, and with all my former trouble lying heavy upon me, disappointment and despair came well nigh being my executioners. In this dilemma, who can imagine my distress when my little son came running to me one morning, swollen with tears, exclaiming that the Indians were going to carry him into the woods to hunt? He had scarcely told the piteous story before his master came to pull him away. He threw his little arms around me, begging, in the agony of grief, that I would keep him. The inexorable savage unclinched his hands and forced him away: the last words I heard, intermingled with his cries, were, "Ma'am, I shall never see you again." The keenness of my pangs almost obliged me to wish that I had never been a mother. "Farewell, Sylvanus," said I; "God will preserve you."

Mr. Johnson and my daughter were taken with the small pox; and I obtained permission to go to the hospital and see them, after which I never returned to the Indians. It is a singular instance of divine inter-position that we all recovered from this malignant disease. We were remanded to prison, but were not compelled to our former rigid confinement. Mr. Johnson was allowed, at certain times, to go about the city in quest of provision. But, on the 20th of October, St. Luc Lucorne arrived from Montreal with the news of Dieskau's defeat: he had, ever since my husband's misfortune about his parole, been his per-secuting enemy. By his instigation we were all put directly to close prison.

The ravages of the small pox reduced us to the last extremity; and the fetid prison, without fire or food, added bitterness to our distress. Mr. Johnson preferred a petition to the lord intendant, stating our mel-ancholy situation. I had the liberty of presenting it myself; and by the assistance of Mr. Perthieur, the interpreter, in whom we ever found a compassionate friend, we got some small relief. About the 1st of No-vember I was taken violently ill of a fever, and was carried to the hospital with my daughter Captive. After a month's residence there, with tol-erably good attendance, I recovered from my illness and went back to my husband. While at the hospital I found an opportunity to convey the unwelcome tidings of our deplorable situation to my sister at Montreal, charging her to give my best love to my daughter Susanna, and to inform our fellow-prisoners, Labarree and Farnsworth, that our good wishes awaited them. Not a word had we yet heard from poor Sylvanus.

Winter now began to approach, and the severe frosts of Canada op-erated keenly upon our feelings. Our prison was a horrid defence from the blasts of December: with two chairs, and a heap of straw, and two lousy blankets, we may well be supposed to live uncomfortably: but in addition to this, we had but one poor fire a day, and the iron grates gave free access to the chills of the inclement sky. A quart basin was the only thing allowed us to cook our small piece of meat and dirty crusts in; and it must serve at the same time for table furniture. In this sad plight,—a prisoner, in jail, winter approaching,—conceive, reader, for I cannot speak, our distress.

Our former benevolent friends, Captains Stowbrow and Vambram, had the peculiar misfortune to be cast into a prison opposite to us. Sus-picion of having corresponded with their countrymen was the crime with which they were charged. Their misfortune did not preclude the exertion of generosity: they frequently sent us, by the waiting maid, bottles of wine and articles of provision. But the malice of Frenchmen had now arrived to such a pitch against all our country that we must be deprived of these comforts. These good men were forbidden their offices of kindness, and our intercourse was entirely prohibited. We, however, found means by a stratagem to effect in some measure what could not be done by open dealing. When the servants were carrying in our daily supplies, we slipped into the entry and deposited our letters in an ash box, which were taken by our friends, they leaving one at the same time for us: this served in some measure to amuse a dull hour. Sometimes we diverted ourselves by the use of Spanish cards: as Mr. Johnson was ignorant of the game, I derived no inconsiderable pleasure from instructing him. But the vigilance of our keepers increased, and our paper and ink were withheld. We had now been prisoners seventeen months, and our prospects were changing from bad to worse. Five months had elapsed since our confinement in this horrid receptacle, except the time we lingered in the hospital. Our jailer was a true descendant from Pharaoh; but, urged by impatience and despair, I softened him so much as to get him to ask Mr. Perthieur to call on us. When the good man came we described our situation in all the moving terms which our feelings inspired, which, in addition to what he saw, convinced him of the reality of our distress. He proposed asking an influential friend of his to call on us, who, perhaps, would devise some mode for our relief. The next day the gentleman came to see us: he was one of those good souls who ever feel for others' woes. He was highly affronted with his countrymen for reducing us to such distress, and declared that the lord intendant himself should call on us and see the extremities to which he had reduced us. He sent from his own house that night a kettle, some candles, and each of us a change of linen.

The next day, January 8, 1756, Mr. Intendant came to see us. He exculpated himself by saying that we were put there by the special order of Monsieur Vaudrieul, the governor-in-chief, and that he had no authority to release us. But he would convey a letter from Mr. Johnson to monsieur, which might have the desired effect. The letter was accordingly written, stating our troubles and beseeching relief; likewise praying that our son might be got from the Indians and sent to us, with our daughter and sister from Montreal. The governor returned the following obliging letter:—

Translation

I have received, sir, your letter, and am much concerned for the situation you are in. I write to Mr. Longieul to put you and your wife in the civil jail. Mr. L. Intendant will be so good as to take some notice of the things you stand in need of, and to help you. As to your boy, who is in the hands of the Indians, I will do all that is in my power to get him; but I do not hope to have a good success in it. Your child in town and your sister-in-law are well. If it is some opportunity of doing you some pleasure I will make use of it, unless some reason might happen that hinder and stop the effects of my good will. If you had not before given some cause of being suspected, you should be at liberty.

I am, sir, your most humble servant,
VAUDRIEUL

From the receipt of this letter we dated our escape from direful bondage. Mr. Intendant ordered us directly to the new jail, called the civil prison, where our accommodations were infinitely better. We had a decent bed, candles, fuel, and all the conveniences belonging to prisoners of war. Mr. Johnson was allowed fifteen pence per day, on account of a lieutenant's commission which he held under George II.; and I was permitted to go once a week into the city to purchase necessaries, and a washerwoman was provided for my use. We were not confined to the narrow limits of a single room, but were restrained only by the bounds of the jail yard. Our situation formed such a contrast with what we endured in the gloomy criminal jail that we imagined ourselves the favorites of fortune and in high life.

Residence in the Civil Jail, and Occurrences till the 20th of July, 1757

To be indolent from necessity has ever been deemed a formidable evil. No better witnesses than ourselves can testify to the truth of the remark, although our lodgings were now such as we envied a month before; yet to be compelled to continual idleness was grievous to be borne. We derived some amusement from the cultivation of a small garden within the jail yard; but a continued sameness of friends and action rendered our time extremely wearisome.

About a month after our arrival at this new abode, one Captain Milton, with his crew, who with their vessel were taken at sea, were brought prisoners of war to the same place. Milton was lodged in our apartment. He had all the rude, boisterous airs of a seaman, without the least trait of a gentleman, which rendered him a very troublesome companion. His impudence was consummate; but that was not the greatest evil: while some new recruits were parading before the prison one day, Milton addressed them in very improper language from our window, which was noticed directly by city authority, who, supposing it to be Mr. Johnson, ordered him into the dungeon. Deeply affected by this new trouble, I again called on my friend Mr. Perthieur, who, after having ascertained the facts, got him released. Mr. Milton was then put into other quarters.

A new jailer, who had an agreeable lady for his wife, now made our situation still more happy. My little daughters played with hers and learned the French language. But my children were some trouble; the eldest, Polly, could slip out into the street under the gate, and often came nigh being lost. I applied to the sentinel, and he kept her within proper bounds.

Captain M'Neil and his brother, from Boston, were brought to us as prisoners. They informed us of the state of politics in our own country, and told us some interesting news about some of our friends at home.

In the morning of the 13th of August, our jailer, with moon eyes, came to congratulate us on the taking of Oswego by the French. We entered little into his spirit of joy, preferring much to hear good news from the other side. We were soon visited by some of the prisoners who had surrendered. Colonel Schuyler was in the number, who, with the gentlemen in his suit, made us a generous present.

The remainder of the summer and fall of 1756 passed off without any sensible variation. We frequently heard from Montreal. My sister was very well situated in the family of the lieutenant governor, and my eldest daughter was caressed by her three mothers. Could I have heard from my son, half my trouble would have ended.

In December I was delivered of a son, who lived but a few hours, and was buried under the Cathedral Church.

In the winter I received a letter from my sister, containing the sad tidings of my father's death, who was killed by Indians on his own farm the preceding June, at the age of fifty-three. Savage vengeance fell heavily upon our family. I had a brother wounded at the same time, who ran to the fort with the spear sticking in his thigh. Too much grief reduced me to a weak condition. I was taken sick and carried to the hospital, where, after a month's lingering illness, I found myself able to return.

The commencement of the year 1757 passed off without a prospect of liberty. Part of our fellow-prisoners were sent to France, but we made no voyage out of the jail yard. About the 1st of May we petitioned Mons. Vaudrieul to permit our sister to come to us. Our prayer was granted; and in May we had the pleasure of seeing her, after an absence of two years. She had supported herself by her needle in the family of the lieutenant governor, where she was treated extremely well, and received a present of four crowns at parting.

Impatient of confinement, we now made another attempt to gain our liberty. Mr. Perthieur conducted us to the house of the lord intendant, to whom we petitioned in pressing terms, stating that we had now been prisoners almost three years, and had suffered every thing but death; and that would be our speedy portion, unless we had relief. His lordship listened with seeming pity, and promised to lay our case before the head man at Montreal and give us an answer in seven days; at the expiration of which time we had a permit to leave the prison. It is not easy to describe the effect of such news; those only who have felt the horrors of confinement can figure to themselves the happiness we enjoyed when breathing once more the air of liberty. We took lodgings in town, where we tarried till the 1st of June, when a cartel ship arrived to carry prisoners to England for an exchange. Mr. Johnson wrote an urgent letter to Mons. Vaudrieul, praying that his family might be included with those who were to take passage. Monsieur wrote a very encouraging letter back, promising that he and his family should sail, and that his daughter, Susanna, should be sent to him. He concluded by congratulating him on his good prospects, and ordering the governor of Quebec to afford us his assistance. This letter was dated June the 27th.

This tide of good fortune almost wiped away the remembrance of three years' adversity. We began our preparations for embarkation with alacrity. Mr. Johnson wrote St. Luc Lucorne for the seven hundred livres due on Mr. Cuyler's order; but his request was, and still is, unsatisfied. This was a period big with every thing propitious and happy. The idea of leaving a country where I had suffered the keenest distress during two months and a half with the savages, been bowed down by every mortification and insult which could arise from the misfortunes of my husband in New England, and where I had spent two years in sickness and despair in a prison too shocking to mentioned, contributed to fill the moment with all the happiness which the benevolent reader will conceive my due after sufferings so intense. To consummate the whole, my daughter was to be returned to my arms who had been absent more than two years. There was a good prospect of our son's being released from the Indians. The whole formed such a lucky combination of fortunate events that the danger of twice crossing the ocean to gain our native shore vanished in a moment. My family were all in the same joyful mood, and hailed the happy day when we should sail for England.

But little did we think that this sunshine of prosperity was so soon to be darkened by the heaviest clouds of misfortune. Three days before the appointed hour for sailing, the ship came down from Montreal without my daughter. In a few moments I met Mr. Perthieur, who told me that counter orders had come, and Mr. Johnson must be retained a prisoner; only my two little daughters, sister, and myself could go. This was calamity indeed. To attempt such a long, wearisome voyage, without money and without acquaintance, and to leave a husband and two children in the hands of enemies, was too abhorrent for reflection. But it was an affair of importance, and required weighty consideration. Accordingly, the next day a solemn council of all the prisoners in the city was held at the coffee house. Colonel Schuyler was president; and after numerous arguments for and against were heard, it was voted, by a large majority, that I should go. I, with hesitation, gave my consent. Some, perhaps, will censure the measure as rash, and others may applaud my courage; but I had so long been accustomed to danger and distress, in the most menacing forms they could assume, that I was now almost insensible to their threats; and this act was not a little biased by desperation. Life could no longer retain its value if lingered out in the inimical regions of Canada. In Europe I should, at least, find friends, if not acquaintance; and among the numerous vessels bound to America I might chance to get a passage. But then, to leave a tender husband, who had so long, at the hazard of his life, preserved my own,—to part, perhaps forever, from two children,—put all my resolution to the test and shook my boasted firmness.

Colonel Schuyler, whom we ever found our benevolent friend, promised to use his influence for Mr. Johnson's release and for the redemption of our children.

On the 20th of July we went on board the vessel, accompanied by Mr. Johnson, who went with us to take leave. We were introduced to the captain, who was a gentleman and a person of great civility. He showed us the best cabin, which was to be the place of our residence; and after promising my husband that the voyage should be made as agreeable to me as possible, he gave orders for weighing anchor. The time was now come that we must part. Mr. Johnson took me by the hand; our tears imposed silence. I saw him step into the barge; but my two little children, sister, and myself were bound for Europe.

We fell down the River St. Lawrence but a small distance that night. The next morning the captain, with a cheerful countenance, came to our cabin and invited us to rise and take our leave of Quebec. None but myself complied; and I gazed, as long as sight would permit, at the place where I had left my dearest friend.

While in the custody of the Canadians, a number of circumstances occurred with which my memory is not strongly impressed; but a dream which I had while in the civil jail will never be forgotten. Methought that I had two rings on one finger; the one a plain, and the other a diamond mourning ring. The plain ring broke and fell from my finger, while the other remained. My family was now broke, and I left to mourn.

Voyage to Plymouth.—Occurrences.—Sailing from Plymouth to Portsmouth; from thence, by the Way of Cork, to New York

All my fears and affliction did not prevent my feeling some little joy at being released from the jurisdiction of Frenchmen. I could pardon the Indians for their vindictive spirit, because they had no claim to the benefits of civilization. But the French, who give lessons of politeness to the rest of the world, can derive no advantage from the plea of ignorance. The blind superstition which is inculcated by their monks and friars doubtless stifles, in some measure, the exertion of pity towards their enemies; and the common herd, which includes almost seven eighths of their number, have no advantages from education. But I found some benevolent friends, whose generosity I shall ever recollect with the warmest gratitude.

The commencement of the voyage had every favorable presage; the weather was fine, the sailors cheerful, and the ship in good trim. My accommodations in the captain's family were very commodious. A boy was allowed me for my particular use. We sailed with excellent fortune till the 19th of August, when we hove in sight of old Plymouth, and at four o'clock in the afternoon dropped anchor.

The next day all but myself and family were taken from the vessel. We felt great anxiety at being left, and began to fear that fortune was not willing to smile on us even on these shores. We waited in despair thirty or forty hours and found no relief. The captain, observing our despondency, began his airs of gayety to cheer us. He assured us that we should not suffer; that, if the English would not receive us, he would take us to France and make us happy. But at last an officer came on board to see if the vessel was prepared for the reception of French prisoners. We related to him our situation. He conducted us on shore and applied to the admiral for directions, who ordered us lodgings and the king's allowance of two shillings sterling per day for our support. Fortunately we were lodged in a house where resided Captain John Tufton Mason, whose name will be familiar to the inhabitants of New Hampshire on account of his patent. He very kindly interested himself in our favor, and wrote to Messrs. Thomlinson and Apthorp, agents at London for the Province of New Hampshire, soliciting their assistance in my behalf. We tarried at Plymouth but a fortnight, during which time I received much attention, and had to gratify many inquisitive friends with the history of my sufferings.

Captain Mason procured me a passage to Portsmouth in the Rainbow man-of-war, from whence I was to take passage in a packet for America. Just as I stepped on board the Rainbow, a good lady, with her son, came to make me a visit. Her curiosity to see a person of my description was not abated by my being on my passage. She said she could not sleep till she had seen the person who had suffered such hard fortune. After she had asked all the questions that time would allow of she gave me a guinea, and a half guinea to my sister, and a muslin handkerchief to each of our little girls. On our arrival at Portsmouth the packet had sailed. The captain of the Rainbow, not finding it convenient to keep us with him, introduced us on board the Royal Ann.

Wherever we lived we found the best friends and the politest treatment. It will be thought singular that a defenceless woman should suffer so many changes without meeting with some insults and many incivilities. But during my long residence on board the various vessels I received the most delicate attention from my companions. The officers were assiduous in making my situation agreeable, and readily proffered their services.

While on board the Royal Ann I received the following letters. The reader will excuse the recitation. It would be ingratitude not to record such conspicuous acts of benevolence.

PLYMOUTH, September 13, 1757

MADAM,—Late last postnight I received an answer from Mr. Apthorp, who is partner with Mr. Thomlinson, the agent for New Hampshire, with a letter enclosed to you, which gave you liberty to draw on him for fifteen guineas. As Madam Hornech was just closing her letter to you, I gave it her to enclose for you. I now write again to London on your behalf. You must immediately write Mr. Apthorp what you intend to do, and what further you would have him and our friends at London do for you.

I hope you have received the benefaction of the charitable ladies in this town. All friends here commiserate your misfortunes and wish you well, together with your sister and children.

Your friend and countryman to serve,
JOHN T. MASON

Mrs. Johnson

LONDON, September 7, 1757

MADAM,—I received a letter from Captain Mason, dated the 30th of last month, giving an account of your unfortunate situation; and yesterday Mr. Thomlinson, who is ill in the country, sent me your letter, together with Captain Mason's, to him, with the papers relative to you. In consequence of which I this day applied to a number of gentlemen in your behalf, who very readily gave their assistance; but as I am a stranger to the steps you intend to pursue, I can only give you liberty at present to draw on me for ten or fifteen guineas, for which sum your bill shall be paid; and when you furnish me with information I shall very cheerfully give any furtherance in my power to your relief, when I shall also send you a list of your benefactors.   I am, madam,

Your most humble servant,

JOHN APTHORP

Mrs. Susanna Johnson

Letter from H. Grove

I have now the pleasure to let dear Mrs. Johnson know the goodness of Mrs. Hornech. She has collected seven pounds for you, and sent it to Mrs. Brett, who lives in the yard at Portsmouth, to beg her favors to you in any thing she can do to help or assist you. She is a good lady: do go to her and let her know your distress. Captain Mason has got a letter this post, but he is not at home; cannot tell you further. You will excuse this scrawl, likewise my not enlarging, as Mr. Hornech waits to send it away. Only believe me, madam, you have my earnest prayers to God to help and assist you. My mamma's compliments with mine, and begs to wait on you; and believe me, dear Mrs. Johnson, yours in all events to serve you,

HANNAH GROVE

Sunday eve, 10 o'clock

I received the donation, and Mr. Apthorp sent me the fifteen guineas. I sincerely lament that he omitted sending me the names of my benefactors.

The captain of the Royal Ann, supposing my situation with him might not be so convenient, applied to the mayor for a permit for me to take lodgings in the city; which was granted. I took new lodgings, where I tarried three or four days, when orders came for me to be on board the Orange man-of-war in three hours, which was to sail for America. We made all possible despatch; but when we got to the shore we were astonished to find the ship too far under way to be overtaken. No time was to be lost. I applied to a waterman to carry us to a merchantman, which was weighing anchor at a distance to go in the same fleet. He hesitated long enough to pronounce a chapter of oaths, and rowed us off. When we came to the vessel I petitioned the captain to take us on board till he overtook the Orange. He directly flew into a violent passion, and offered greater insults than I had ever received during my whole voyage. He swore we were women of bad fame, who wished to follow the army, and that he would have nothing to do with us. I begged him to calm his rage, and we would convince him of his error. But fortunately the victualler of the fleet happened to be in the ship, who at this moment stepped forward with his roll of names and told the outrageous captain that he would soon convince him whether we deserved notice by searching his list. He soon found our names, and the captain began to beg pardon. He took us on board and apologized for his rudeness.

When within half a dozen miles of Springfield, Mr. Ely, a benevolent friend of Mr. Johnson's, sent his two sons with a sleigh to convey me to his house, where I proposed staying till some of my friends could hear of my arrival. Fortunately Mr. Johnson about the same time arrived at Boston; but misfortune had not yet filled the measure of his calamity. He had no sooner landed than he was put under guard, on suspicion of not performing his duty in the redemption of the Canada prisoners, which suspicion was occasioned by his remissness in producing his vouchers. But the following certificate procured his liberty:—

This is to certify whom it may concern, that the bearer, Lieutenant James Johnson, inhabitant in the town of Charlestown, in the Province of New Hampshire, in New England, who, together with his family, were taken by the Indians on the 30th of August, 1754, has ever since continued a steady and faithful subject to his majesty King George, and has used his utmost endeavors to redeem his own family, and all others belonging to the province aforesaid, that were in the hands of the French and Indians, which he cannot yet accomplish; and that both himself and family have undergone innumerable hardships and afflictions since they have been prisoners in Canada.

In testimony of which, we, the subscribers, officers in his Britannic majesty's service, and now prisoners of war at Quebec, have thought it necessary to grant him this certificate, and do recommend him as an object worthy the aid and compassion of every honest Englishman.

(Signed,)
PETER SCHUYLER
ANDREW WATKINS
WILLIAM MARTIN
WILLIAM PADGETT

QUEBEC, September 16, 1757

To compensate him for this misfortune, Governor Pownall recommended a grant, which the general court complied with, and gave him one hundred dollars from the treasury; and he was recorded a faithful subject of King George.

After his dismission from the guards in Boston he proceeded directly for Charlestown. When within fifteen miles of Springfield he was met by a gentleman who had just before seen me, who gave him the best news he could have heard: although it was then late at night, he lost not a moment. At two o'clock in the morning of the 1st of January, 1758, I again embraced my dearest friend. Happy New Year! With pleasure would I describe my emotions of joy, could language paint them sufficiently forcible; but the feeble pen shrinks from the task.

Charlestown was still a frontier town, and suffered from savage depredations, which rendered it an improper residence for me; consequently I went to Lancaster. Mr. Johnson in a few days set out for New York to adjust his Canada accounts. But on his journey he was persuaded by Governor Pownall to take a captain's commission and join the forces bound for Ticonderoga, where he was killed on the 8th of July following, in the battle that proved fatal to Lord How, while fighting for his country. Humanity will weep with me. The cup of sorrow was now replete with bitter drops. All my former miseries were lost in the affliction of a widow.

In October, 1758, I was informed that my son Sylvanus was at Northampton sick of a scald. I hastened to the place and found him in a deplorable situation. He was brought there by Major Putnam, (afterwards General Putnam,) with Mrs. How and her family, who had returned from captivity. The town of Northampton had taken the charge of him. His situation was miserable: when I found him he had no recollection of me; but after some conversation he had some confused ideas of me, but no remembrance of his father. It was four years since I had seen him; he was then eleven years old. During his absence he had entirely forgotten the English language, spoke a little broken French, but was perfect in Indian. He had been with the savages three years, and one year with the French; but his habits were somewhat Indian. He had been with them in their hunting excursions and suffered numerous hardships; he could brandish a tomahawk or bend the bow; but these habits wore off by degrees. I carried him from that place to Lancaster, where he lived a few years with Colonel Aaron Willard.

I lived in Lancaster till October, 1759, when I returned to old Charlestown. The sight of my former residence afforded a strange mixture of joy and grief; while the desolations of war, and the loss of a number of dear and valuable friends, combined to give the place an air of melancholy. Soon after my arrival Major Rogers returned from an expedition against the village of St. Francis, which he had destroyed, and killed most of the inhabitants. He brought with him a young Indian prisoner, who stopped at my house: the moment he saw me he cried, "My God! my God! here is my sister!" It was my little brother Sabatis, who formerly used to bring the cows for me when I lived at my Indian masters. He was transported to see me, and declared that he was still my brother, and I must be his sister. Poor fellow! The fortune of war had left him without a single relation; but with his country's enemies he could find one who too sensibly felt his miseries. I felt the purest pleasure in administering to his comfort.

I was extremely fortunate in receiving, by one of Major Rogers's men, a bundle of Mr. Johnson's papers, which he found in pillaging St. Francis. The Indians took them when we were captivated, and they had lain at St. Francis five years.

Sabatis went from Charlestown to Crown Point with Major Rogers. When he got to Otter Creek he met my son Sylvanus, who was in the army with Colonel Willard. He recognized him, and, clasping him in his arms, "My God!" says he, "the fortune of war!" I shall ever remember this young Indian with affection: he had a high sense of honor and good behavior: he was affable, good natured, and polite.

My daughter Susanna was still in Canada; but as I had the fullest assurances that every attention was paid to her education and welfare by her three mothers, I felt less anxiety than I otherwise might have done.

Every one will imagine that I have paid Affliction her utmost demand: the pains of imprisonment, the separation from my children, the keen sorrow occasioned by the death of a butchered father, and the severe grief arising from my husband's death, will amount to a sum perhaps unequalled. But still my family must be doomed to further and severe persecutions from the savages. In the commencement of the summer of 1766, my brother-in-law, Mr. Joseph Willard, son of the Rev. Mr. Willard, of Rutland, who was killed by the Indians in Lovell's war, with his wife and five children, who lived but two miles distant from me, were taken by a party of Indians. They were carried much the same route that I was to Montreal. Their journey of fourteen days through wilderness was a series of miseries unknown to any but those who have suffered Indian captivity: they lost two children, whose deaths were owing to savage barbarity. The history of their captivity would almost equal my own; but the reader's commiseration and pity must now be exhausted. No more of anguish; no more of sufferings.

They arrived at Montreal a few days before the French surrendered it to the English, and after four months' absence returned home, and brought my daughter Susanna to my arms. While I rejoiced at again meeting my child, whom I had not seen for above five years, I felt extremely grateful to the Mrs. Jaissons for the affectionate attention they had bestowed on her. As they had received her as their child, they had made their affluent fortune subservient to her best interest. To give her the accomplishments of a polite education had been their principal care: she had contracted an ardent love for them, which never will be obliterated. Their parting was an affecting scene of tears. They never forgot her during their lives: she has eight letters from them, which are proofs of the warmest friendship. My daughter did not know me at her return, and spoke nothing but French: my son spoke Indian; so that my family was a mixture of nations.

Mr. Farnsworth, my only fellow-prisoner whose return I have not mentioned, came home a little before.

Thus, by the goodness of Providence, we all returned in the course of six painful years to the place from whence we were taken. The long period of our captivity and the severity of our sufferings will be called uncommon and unprecedented. But we even found some friends to pity among our most persecuting enemies; and from the various shapes in which mankind appeared, we learned many valuable lessons. Whether in the wilds of Canada, the horrid jails of Quebec, or in our voyage to Europe, daily occurrences happened to convince us that the passions of men are as various as their complexions. And although my sufferings were often increased by the selfishness of this world's spirit, yet the numerous testimonies of generosity I received bid me suppress the charge of neglect or want of benevolence. That I have been an unfortunate woman, all will grant; yet my misfortunes, while they enriched my experience and taught me the value of patience, have increased my gratitude to the Author of all blessings, whose goodness and mercy have preserved my life to the present time.

During the time of my widowhood, misfortune and disappointment were my intimate companions. When New England was ruled by a few men who were the creatures of the king, the pleasures of dissipation were preferred to the more severe attention to business; and the small voice of a woman was seldom heard. Hence, in the settlement of my husband's estate, the delay and perplexity were distressing. I made three journeys to Portsmouth, fourteen to Boston, and three to Springfield, to effect the settlement. Whether my captivity had taught me to be ungrateful, or whether imagination formed a catalogue of evils, I will not pretend to say; but from the year 1754 to the present day, greater misfortunes have apparently fallen to my share than to mankind in general, and the meteor happiness has eluded my grasp. The life of a widow is peculiarly afflictive; but my numerous and long journeys over roads imminently bad, and incidents that seemed to baffle all my plans and foresight, render mine more unfortunate than common.

But I found many attentive friends, whose assistance and kindness will always claim my gratitude. Colonel White, of Leominster, with whom I had lived from the time I was eight years old until I married, was extremely affectionate and kind: in his house I found a welcome home. Mr. Samuel Ely, of Springfield, who was the friend of my husband, rendered me numerous kindnesses. Colonel Murray, of Rutland, and Colonel Chandler, of Worcester, were very friendly and kind. Mr. Clarke, deputy secretary, Governor Pownall, and Governor Wentworth, exerted their influence for me in attempting to procure a grant from the general assembly.

In one of my journeys to Portsmouth I conversed with Captain Adams, who was in Europe at the time I was. He informed me that while there Mr. Apthorp gave him fourteen pounds sterling, for the purpose of conveying me and my family to America. My sailing with the convoy prevented my receiving this kindness.

During the four years of my widowhood I was in quite an unsettled situation; sometimes receiving my children who were returning from captivity, and others settling the estate of my deceased husband. In October, 1759, I moved to Charlestown and took possession of my patrimony, consisting of a house which Colonel Whiting had generously assisted my mother in building. In copartnership with my brother, Moses Willard, I kept a small store, which was of service in supporting my family and settling my husband's estate. I have received, by petitioning, from the general assembly of New Hampshire forty-two pounds, to indemnify myself and family for losses sustained by our country's enemies. This was of eminent service to me. Mr. Johnson left with Mr. Charles Apthorp, of Boston, the sum which my son's redemption cost, for Colonel Schuyler, who had paid the same. But the general assembly of Massachusetts afterwards paid Colonel Schuyler his demand for redeeming my son.

By Mr. Johnson I had seven children: two sons and a daughter died in infancy. Sylvanus, with whom the reader is acquainted, now lives in Charlestown. Susanna married Captain Samuel Wetherbee, and has been the mother of fifteen children, among whom were five at two births. Polly married Colonel Timothy Bedel, of Haverhill: she died in August, 1789. Captive married Colonel George Kimball. In the year 1762 I married Mr. John Hastings, my present husband. He was one of the first settlers in Charlestown. I recollect to have seen him when I visited the place in the year 1744. He suffered much by the Indians, and assisted in defending the town during the wars. By him I have had seven children: one daughter and four sons died in their infancy. Theodosia is married to Mr. Stephen Hasham. Randilla died at the age of twenty-two. She lived from her infancy with Mr. Samuel Taylor, of Rockingham, by whom she was treated with great affection. I have had thirty-nine grandchildren and four great-grandchildren.

I am now in the winter of life, and feel sensibly the effects of old age. I live on the same spot where the Indians took us from in 1754; but the face of Nature has so changed that old savage fears are all banished. My vacant hours I often employ in reflecting on the various scenes that have marked the different stages of my life. When viewing the present rising generation, in the bloom of health and enjoying those gay pleasures which shed their exhilarating influence so plentifully in the morn of life, I look back to my early days, when I, too, was happy and basked in the sunshine of good fortune. Little do they think that the meridian of their lives can possibly be rendered miserable by captivity or a prison: as little, too, did I think that my gilded prospects could be obscured: but it was the happy delusion of youth; and I fervently wish there was no deception. But that Being who "sits upon the circle of the earth and views the inhabitants as grasshoppers" allots all our fortunes.

Although I have drunk so largely from the cup of sorrow, yet my present happiness is a small compensation. Twice has my country been ravaged by war since my remembrance. I have detailed the share I bore in the first: in the last, although the place in which I live was not a field of bloody battle, yet its vicinity to Ticonderoga and the savages that ravaged the Coos country rendered it perilous and distressing. But now no one can set a higher value on the smiles of peace than myself. The savages are driven beyond the lakes, and our country has no enemies. The gloomy wilderness, that forty years ago secreted the Indian and the beast of prey, has vanished away, and the thrifty farm smiles in its stead; the Sundays, that were then employed in guarding a fort, are now quietly devoted to worship; the tomahawk and scalping knife have given place to the sickle and ploughshare; and prosperous husbandry now thrives where the terrors of death once chilled us with fear.

My numerous progeny often gather around me to hear the sufferings once felt by their aunt or grandmother, and wonder at their magnitude. My daughter Captive still keeps the dress she appeared in when brought to my bedside by the French nurse at the Ticonderoga hospital, and often refreshes my memory with past scenes when showing it to her children. These things yield a kind of melancholy pleasure.

Instances of longevity are remarkable in my family. My aged mother, before her death, could say to me, "Arise, daughter, and go to thy daughter; for thy daughter's daughter has got a daughter;" a command which few mothers can make and be obeyed.

And now, reader, after sincerely wishing that your days may be as happy as mine have been unfortunate, I bid you adieu.

CHARLESTOWN, June 20, 1798

Names of Persons Killed by the Indians in Charlestown, No. 4

Seth Putnam, May 2, 1748
Samuel Farnsworth ⎫
Joseph Allen   ⎪
Peter Perin   ⎬ May 24, 1746
Aaron Lyon   ⎪
Joseph Massey   ⎭
Jedediah Winchel, June or July, 1746
———— Philips, August 3, 1746
Isaac Goodale   ⎫ October, 1747
Nathaniel Gould ⎭
Obadiah Sartwell, June, 1749
Lieutenant Moses Willard, June 18, 1756
Asahel Stebbins, August, 1758
Josiah Kellogg, 1759

Number taken Prisoners by the Indians from Charlestown, No. 4

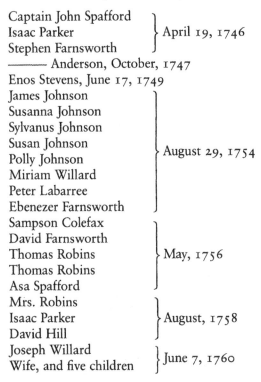

Captain John Spafford ⎫
Isaac Parker   ⎬ April 19, 1746
Stephen Farnsworth   ⎭
——— Anderson, October, 1747
Enos Stevens, June 17, 1749
James Johnson ⎫
Susanna Johnson │
Sylvanus Johnson │
Susan Johnson   ⎬ August 29, 1754
Polly Johnson   │
Miriam Willard   │
Peter Labarree   │
Ebenezer Farnsworth ⎭
Sampson Colefax ⎫
David Farnsworth │
Thomas Robins   ⎬ May, 1756
Thomas Robins   │
Asa Spafford   ⎭
Mrs. Robins   ⎫
Isaac Parker   ⎬ August, 1758
David Hill   ⎭
Joseph Willard   ⎫ June 7, 1760
Wife, and five children ⎭

[from *Indian Narratives: Containing a Correct and Interesting History of the Indian Wars, from the Landing of Our Pilgrim Fathers, 1620 to Gen. Wayne's Victory, 1794* (Claremont, N.H.: Tracy and Brothers, 1854), 128–82.]

Narrative of James Johnson

Deposition of Captain Johnson

THE COMMITTEE who was directed to examine James Johnson, a Late Captain in Canada, beg leave to Report that he gives ye following account of facts (viz.) that it is a hundred miles from No. 4 to Crown Point that in his Journey to Canada he passed a River Called black River ye

first night that he Crossed White River Several times and for want of a
canoe he travel'd by otter Creek that in General the travelling was good
that he could not tell how high the Emminence of Crown Point was but
that the Citadel is the opposite side & before (.) ye breastwork was
Raised Shot would strike ye Door of ye Citadel from ye Emminence &
the wall of the fort is twelve feet high & twelve feet thick & then abreast
work about Two foot thickness—(the) heights & ye Cannon are planted
nearly alike Round the fort Excepting on part of ye north Square where
ye barracks are (&) that there is no out works (&) that he apprehends
the Citadel is not tenable against proper battering pieces and that the
place of unloading their vessell from the fort is about Sixty Rod & the
Emminence is a hundred Rod from ye place of unloading & before ye
vessell Can be Covered by ye fort She must be Exposed to a fire from
ye Emminence & that ye powder house Stores exposed to ye Emminence
that there is no no well in ye fort that ye Store house is next to the
Emminence that there is but one outer Gate & that has a Drawbridge
before it & a Gate within that, which may be drawn up (&) drop'd
down as occasion Requires that there is no (?) in ye fort & but one vessel
in ye lake which is about 70 tons without guns & that from Crown
Point he went to St Johns Fort at the other end of ye Lake and from there
to Champlain River & that from St Johns Fort to St Francis is about fifty
miles near north & from St Francis to St Lawrence is about five miles &
that ye Rout between St Johns and St Francis there are two Rows of
houses one on each side ye River in the whole about two hundred in
some places pretty thick & a fort at Chamblain as Strong as Crown
Point & that the whole village of St Francis Stands on an rise of Ground
Mountains near fourty buildings of all Sorts that there is no fort in it
but some stone houses and buildings no considerable Settlements within
fifteen miles of S Francis neither did he hear of any & he apprehended
there is no settlement near than Tres Riveres which is about fifteen miles
from S Francis and that there is of St Francis & Shatacooks about one
hundred & Twenty fighting men that S Francis Lyes on ye north side
the River of that Name & her three great Guns not mounted which they
fire on Some occasion that there is young woods about the Town on ye
East & north sides & that he apprehends the Distance to Mount Royal
from St Francis about fifty miles Southwest Southerly & that Mt Royal
is Walled all Round about twelve feet high about Same thickness of
Crown Point & and as is about as big as Charlestown that the Town is
built Long & narrow and has many Gates to it that there are on that
Island four or five hundred houses Twenty seven Cannon & two mortars
all planted on a little hill within the walls and that he saw about Twenty

vessels in Quebeck River at one time which were a kind of Brigantines and that during his Tarrying at St Francis which was about three weeks the French carried meat at most Every day & Distributed it among the Indians and as they took no account of it nore made any Reconing about it he apprehended it Sent from the Government and also he saw five barrels of powder & some balls and Coats which the Indians told him the French gave them and that at Tres Riveres there is a Furnace where they Cast Great Guns & that fourty men were Sent from old France for that purpose. By order

JOHN CHOATE

[from G. Waldo Browne, ed., *Narrative of James Johnson. A Captive During the Indian Wars in New England.* Compiled from the Massachusetts Archives, vol. 38: 329 (Manchester, N.H., 1902), 4–6.]

JEMIMA HOWE

Jemima Howe was born in 1722 or 1723. Her first husband, William Phipps, was killed by Indians at the beginning of King George's War. A year later she married Caleb Howe, a son of Nehemiah How. Indians killed her second husband and took her captive in 1755. Colonel Peter Schuyler of New York took an interest in securing her ransom and New Hampshire paid it: "Nov. 1— 1758—pd. for Mrs. Jem: How 600 livres her son William 800, her sons, Squire & Caleb 1200 paid Sundry Expnss 170." After her return from captivity, Jemima married Colonel Amos Tute. The Reverend Bunker Gay, to whom she told the story of her captivity and who communicated it to Jeremy Belknap for his History, *wrote the following epitaph:*

Mrs. Jemima Tute

Successively Relict of Messrs
William Phipps, Caleb Howe & Amos Tute
The two first were killed by the Indians
Phipps July 5th 1743
Howe June 29th 1755
When Howe was killed, she & her Children
Then seven in number
Were carried into Captivity
The oldest a Daughter went to France
The youngest was torn from her Breast
And perished with Hunger
By the aid of some benevolent Gentn
And her own personal Heroism
She recovered the rest
She had two by her last Husband
Outlived both him & them
And died March 7th 1805 aged 82
Having passed thro more vicissitudes
And endured more hardships
Than any of her contemporaries

[Coleman, *New England Captives Carried to Canada* 2: 314–19; "The Irresistible Mrs. Howe," in Howard H. Peckham, *Captured by Indians: True Tales of Pioneer Survivors* (New Brunswick, N.J.: Rutgers University Press, 1954), 50–61.]

The Captivity and Sufferings of
Mrs. Jemima Howe

Taken prisoner by the Indians at Bridgman's Fort, in the present town of Vernon, Vt. Communicated to Dr. Belknap by the Rev. Bunker Gay, 1755

As MESSRS. Caleb Howe, Hilkiah Grout, and Benjamin Gaffield, who had been hoeing corn in the meadow, west of the river, were returning home a little before sunset, to a place called Bridgman's Fort, they were fired upon by twelve Indians, who had ambushed their path. Howe was on horseback, with two young lads, his children, behind him. A ball, which broke his thigh, brought him to the ground. His horse ran a few rods, and fell likewise, and both the lads were taken. The Indians, in their savage manner, coming up to Howe, pierced his body with a spear, tore off his scalp, stuck a hatchet in his head, and left him in this forlorn condition. He was found alive the morning after by a party of men from Fort Hinsdale; and being asked by one of the party whether he knew him,, he answered, "Yes, I know you all." These were his last words, though he did not expire until after his friends had arrived with him at Fort Hinsdale. Grout was so fortunate as to escape unhurt; but Gaffield, in attempting to wade through the river, at a certain place which was indeed fordable at that time, was unfortunately drowned. Flushed with the success they had met with here, the savages went directly to Bridgman's Fort. There was no man in it, and only three women and some children, viz., Mrs. Jemima Howe, Mrs. Submit Grout, and Mrs. Eunice Gaffield. Their husbands I need not mention again, and their feelings at this juncture I will not attempt to describe. They had heard the enemy's guns, but knew not what had happened to their friends. Extremely anxious for their safety, they stood longing to embrace them, until at length, concluding from the noise they heard without that some of them were come, they unbarred the gate in a hurry to receive them; when, lo! to their inexpressible disappointment and surprise, instead of their husbands, in rushed a number of hideous Indians, to whom they and their tender offspring became an easy prey, and from whom they had nothing to expect but either an immediate death or a long and doleful captivity.

The latter of these, by the favor of Providence, turned out to be the lot of these unhappy women, and their still more unhappy, because more helpless, children. Mrs. Gaffield had but one, Mrs. Grout had three, and Mrs. Howe seven. The eldest of Mrs. Howe's was eleven years old, and the youngest but six months. The two eldest were daughters which she had by her first husband, Mr. William Phipps, who was also slain by the Indians. It was from the mouth of this woman that I lately received the foregoing account. She also gave me, I doubt not, a true, though, to be sure, a very brief and imperfect history of her captivity, which I here insert for your perusal. It may perhaps afford you some amusement, and can do no harm, if, after it has undergone your critical inspection, you should not think it (or an abbreviation of it) worthy to be preserved among the records you are about to publish.

The Indians (she says) having plundered and put fire to the fort, we marched, as near as I could judge, a mile and a half into the woods, where we encamped that night. When the morning came, and we had advanced as much farther, six Indians were sent back to the place of our late abode, who collected a little more plunder, and destroyed some other effects that had been left behind; but they did not return until the day was so far spent that it was judged best to continue where we were through the night. Early the next morning we set off for Canada, and continued our march eight days successively, until we had reached the place where the Indians had left their canoes, about fifteen miles from Crown Point. This was a long and tedious march; but the captives, by divine assistance, were enabled to endure it with less trouble and difficulty than they had reason to expect. From such savage masters, in such indigent circumstances, we could not rationally hope for kinder treatment than we received. Some of us, it is true, had a harder lot than others; and, among the children, I thought my son Squire had the hardest of any. He was then only four years old; and when we stopped to rest our weary limbs, and he sat down on his master's pack, the savage monster would often knock him off, and sometimes, too, with the handle of his hatchet. Several ugly marks, indented in his head by the cruel Indians at that tender age, are still plainly to be seen.

At length we arrived at Crown Point, and took up our quarters there for the space of near a week. In the mean time some of the Indians went to Montreal, and took several of the weary captives along with them, with a view of selling them to the French. They did not succeed, however, in finding a market for any of them. They gave my youngest daughter, Submit Phipps, to the governor, De Vaudreuil, had a drunken frolic, and returned again to Crown Point, with the rest of their prisoners. From hence we set off for St. John's, in four or five canoes, just as night was coming on, and were soon surrounded with darkness. A heavy storm hung over us. The sound of the rolling thunder was very terrible upon the waters, which, at every flash of expansive lightning, seemed to be all in a blaze. Yet to this we were indebted for all the light we enjoyed. No object could we discern any longer than the flashes lasted. In this posture we sailed in our open, tottering canoes almost the whole of that dreary night. The morning, indeed, had not yet begun to dawn, when we all went ashore; and, having collected a heap of sand and gravel for a pillow, I laid myself down, with my tender infant by my side, not knowing where any of my other children were, or what a miserable condition they might be in. The next day, however, under the wing of that ever-present and all-powerful Providence which had preserved us through the darkness and imminent dangers of the preceding night, we all arrived in safety at St. John's.

Our next movement was to St. Francis, the metropolis, if I may so call it, to which the Indians who led us captive belonged. Soon after our arrival at their wretched capital, a council, consisting of the chief sachem and some principal warriors of the St. Francis tribe, was convened; and after the ceremonies usual on such occasions were over, I was conducted and delivered to an old squaw, whom the Indians told me I must call my mother—my infant still continuing to be the property of its original Indian owners. I was nevertheless permitted to keep it with me a while longer, for the sake of saving them the trouble of looking after it, and of maintaining it with my milk. When the weather began to grow cold, shuddering at the prospect of approaching winter, I acquainted my new mother that I did not think it would be possible for me to endure it if I must spend it with her, and fare as the Indians did. Listening to my repeated and earnest solicitations that I might be disposed of among some of the French inhabitants of Canada, she at length set off with me and my infant, attended by some male Indians, upon a journey to Montreal, in hopes of finding a market for me there. But the attempt proved unsuccessful, and the journey tedious indeed. Our provisions were so scanty, as well as insipid and unsavory, the weather was so cold, and the travelling so very bad, that it often seemed as if I must have perished on the way. The lips of my poor child were sometimes so benumbed that when I put it to my breast, it could not, till it grew warm, imbibe the nourishment requisite for its support. While we were at Montreal, we went into the house of a certain French gentleman, whose lady, being sent for, and coming into the room where I was, to examine me, seeing I had an infant, exclaimed suddenly in this manner: *"Damn it, I will not buy a woman that has a child to look after."* There was a swill pail standing near me, in which I observed some crusts and crumbs of bread swimming on the surface of the greasy liquor it contained. Sorely pinched with hunger, I skimmed them off with my hands, and ate them; and this was all the refreshment which the house afforded me. Somewhere, in the course of this visit to Montreal, my Indian mother was so unfortunate as to catch the small pox, of which distemper she died, soon after our return, which was by water, to St. Francis.

And now came on the season when the Indians began to prepare for a winter's hunt. I was ordered to return my poor child to those of them who still claimed it as their property. This was a severe trial. The babe clung to my bosom with all its might; but I was obliged to pluck it thence, and deliver it, shrieking and screaming, enough to penetrate a heart of stone, into the hands of those unfeeling wretches, whose tender mercies may be termed cruel. It was soon carried off by a hunting party of those Indians to a place called Messiskow, at the lower end of Lake Champlain, whither, in about a month after, it was my fortune to follow them. I had preserved my milk, in hopes of seeing my beloved child again; and here I found it, it is true, but in a condition that afforded me no great satisfaction, it being greatly emaciated and almost starved. I took it in my arms, put its face to mine, and it instantly bit me with such violence that it seemed as if I must have parted with a piece of my cheek. I was permitted to lodge with it that and the two following nights; but every morning that intervened, the Indians, I suppose on purpose to torment me, sent me away to another wigwam, which stood at a little distance, though not so far from the one in which my distressed infant was confined but that I could plainly hear its incessant cries and heart-rending lamentations. In this deplorable condition I was obliged to take my leave of it, on the morning of the third day after my arrival at the place. We moved down the lake several miles the same day; and the night following was remarkable on account of the *great earthquake,* which terribly shook that howling wilderness. Among the islands hereabout we spent the winter season, often shifting our quarters, and roving about from one place to another, our family consisting of three persons only, besides myself, viz.: my late mother's daughter, whom, therefore, I called my sister, her sanhop, and a pappoose. They once left me alone two dismal nights; and when they returned to me again, perceiving them smile at each other, I asked, "What is the matter?" They replied that two of my children were no more; one of which, they said, died a natural death, and the other was knocked on the head. I did not utter many words, but my heart was sorely pained within me, and my mind exceedingly troubled with strange and awful ideas. I often imagined, for instance, that I plainly saw the naked carcasses of my deceased children hanging upon the limbs of the trees, as the Indians are wont to hang the raw hides of those beasts which they take in hunting.

It was not long, however, before it was so ordered by kind Providence that I should be relieved in a good measure from those horrid imaginations; for, as I was walking one day upon the ice, observing a smoke at some distance upon the land, it must proceed, thought I, from the fire of some Indian hut; and who knows but some one of my poor children may be there? My curiosity, thus excited, led me to the place, and there I found my son Caleb, a little boy between two and three years old, whom I had lately buried, in sentiment at least, or, rather, imagined to have been deprived of life, and perhaps also denied a decent grave. I found him likewise in tolerable health and circumstances, under the protection of a fond Indian mother; and, moreover, had the happiness of lodging with him in my arms one joyful night. Again we shifted our quarters, and when we had travelled eight or ten miles upon the snow and ice, came to a place where the Indians manufactured sugar, which they extracted from the maple trees. Here an Indian came to visit us, whom I knew, and could speak English. He asked me why I did not go to see my son Squire. I replied that I had lately been informed that he was dead. He assured me that he was yet alive, and but two or three miles off, on the opposite side of the lake. At my request he gave me the best directions he could to the place of his abode. I resolved to embrace the first opportunity that offered of endeavoring to search it out. While I was busy in contemplating this affair, the Indians obtained a little bread, of which they gave me a small share. I did not taste a morsel of it myself, but saved it all for my poor child, if I should be so lucky as to find him. At length, having obtained from my keepers leave to be absent for one day, I set off early in the morning, and steering as well as I could, according to the directions which the friendly Indian had given me, I quickly found the place which he had so accurately marked out. I beheld, as I drew nigh, my little son without the camp; but he looked, thought I, like a starved and mangy puppy, that had been wallowing in the ashes. I took him in my arms, and he spoke to me these words, in the Indian tongue: *"Mother, are you come?"* I took him into the wigwam with me, and observing a number of Indian children in it, I distributed all the bread which I had reserved for my own child among them all, otherwise I should have given great offence. My little boy appeared to be very fond of his new mother, kept as near me as possible while I staid, and when I told him I must go, he fell as though he had been knocked down with a club. But, having recommended him to the care of Him that made him, when the day was far spent, and the time would permit me to stay no longer, I departed, you may well suppose with a heavy load at my heart. The tidings I had received of the death of my youngest child had, a little before, been confirmed to me beyond a doubt; but I could not mourn so heartily for the deceased as for the living child.

When the winter broke up, we removed to St. John's; and through the ensuing summer our principal residence was at no great distance from the fort at that place. In the mean time, however, my sister's husband, having been out with a scouting party to some of the English settlements, had a drunken frolic at the fort when he returned. His wife, who never got drunk, but had often experienced the ill effects of her husband's intemperance, fearing what the consequence might prove if he should come home in a morose and turbulent humor, to avoid his insolence, proposed that we should both retire, and keep out of the reach of it until the storm abated. We absconded, accordingly; but it so happened that I returned and ventured into his presence before his wife had presumed to come nigh him. I found him in his wigwam, and in a surly mood; and not being able to revenge upon his wife, because she was not at home, he laid hold of me, and hurried me to the fort, and, for a trifling consideration, sold me to a French gentleman whose name was Saccapee. "'Tis an ill wind certainly that blows nobody any good." I had been with the Indians a year lacking fourteen days; and if not for my sister, yet for me 'twas a lucky circumstance indeed which thus at last, in an unexpected moment, snatched me out of their cruel hands, and placed me beyond the reach of their insolent power.

After my Indian master had disposed of me in the manner related above, and the moment of sober reflection had arrived, perceiving that the man who bought me had taken the advantage of him in an unguarded hour, his resentment began to kindle, and his indignation rose so high that he threatened to kill me if he should meet me alone, or, if he could not revenge himself thus, that he would set fire to the fort. I was therefore secreted in an upper chamber, and the fort carefully guarded, until his wrath had time to cool. My service in the family to which I was now advanced was perfect freedom in comparison of what it had been among the barbarous Indians. My new master and mistress were both as kind and generous towards me as I could any ways expect. I seldom asked a favor of either of them but it was readily granted; in consequence of which I had it in my power in many instances to administer aid and refreshment to the poor prisoners of my own nation who were brought into St. John's during my abode in the family of the above-mentioned benevolent and hospitable Saccapee. Yet even in this family such trials awaited me as I had little reason to expect; but I stood in need of a large stock of prudence to enable me to encounter them. Must I tell you, then, that even the good old man himself, who considered me as his property, and likewise a warm and resolute son of his, at that same time, and under the same roof, became both excessively fond of my company? so that between these two rivals—the father and the son—I found myself in a very critical situation indeed, and was greatly embarrassed and per-plexed, hardly knowing many times how to behave in such a manner as at once to secure my own virtue and the good esteem of the family in which I resided, and upon which I was wholly dependent for my daily support. At length, however, through the tender compassion of a certain English gentleman, the governor, De Vaudreuil, being made acquainted with the condition I had fallen into, immediately ordered the young and amorous Saccapee, then an officer in the French army, from the field of Venus to the field of Mars, and at the same time also wrote a letter to his father, enjoining it upon him by no means to suffer me to be abused, but to make my situation and service in his family as easy and delightful as possible. I was, moreover, under unspeakable obligations to the gov-ernor upon another account. I had received intelligence from my daugh-ter Mary, the purport of which was, that there was a prospect of her being shortly married to a young Indian of the tribe of St. Francis, with which tribe she had continued from the beginning of her captivity. These were heavy tidings, and added greatly to the poignancy of my other af-flictions. However, not long after I had heard this melancholy news, an opportunity presented of acquainting that humane and generous gentle-man, the commander-in-chief, and my illustrious benefactor, with this affair also, who, in compassion for my sufferings, and to mitigate my sorrows, issued his orders in good time, and had my daughter taken away from the Indians, and conveyed to the same nunnery where her sister was then lodged, with his express injunction that they should both of them together be well looked after and carefully educated, as his adopted children. In this school of superstition and bigotry they con-tinued while the war in those days between France and Great Britain lasted; at the conclusion of which war the governor went home to France, took my oldest daughter along with him, and married her to a French gentleman, whose name is Cron Louis. He was at Boston with the fleet under Count d'Estaing, (1778,) as one of his clerks. My other daughter still continuing in the nunnery, a considerable time had elapsed after my return from captivity, when I made a journey to Canada, re-

solving to use my best endeavors not to return without her. I arrived
just in time to prevent her being sent to France. She was to have gone in
the next vessel that sailed for that place; and I found it extremely difficult
to prevail with her to quit the nunnery and go home with me; yea, she
absolutely refused; and all the persuasions and arguments I could use
with her were to no effect until after I had been to the governor and
obtained a letter from him to the superintendent of the nuns, in which
he threatened, if my daughter should not be immediately delivered into
my hands, or could not be prevailed with to submit to my maternal
authority, that he would send a band of soldiers to assist me in bringing
her away. Upon hearing this, she made no further resistance; but so extremely bigoted was she to the customs and religion of the place, that,
after all, she left it with the greatest reluctance and the most bitter lamentations, which she continued as we passed the streets, and wholly refused to be comforted. My good friend, Major Small, whom we met
with on the way, tried all he could to console her, and was so very kind
and obliging as to bear us company, and carry my daughter behind him
on horseback.

But I have run on a little before my story, for I have not yet informed
you of the means and manner of my own redemption, to the accom-
plishing of which, the recovery of my daughter, just mentioned, and the
ransoming of some of my other children, several gentlemen of note contributed not a little; to whose goodness, therefore, I am greatly indebted,
and sincerely hope I shall never be so ungrateful as to forget. Colonel
Schuyler, in particular, was so very kind and generous as to advance two
thousand seven hundred livres to procure a ransom for myself and three
of my children. He accompanied and conducted us from Montreal to
Albany, and entertained us in the most friendly and hospitable manner
a considerable time at his own house, and I believe entirely at his own
expense.

I have spun out the above narrative to a much greater length than I
at first intended, and shall conclude it with referring you for a more
ample and *brilliant* account of the captive heroine who is the subject of
it to Colonel Humphrey's History of the Life of General Israel Putnam,
together with some remarks upon a few clauses in it. I never indeed had
the pleasure of perusing the whole of said history, but remember to have
seen, some time ago, an extract from it in one of the Boston newspapers,
in which the colonel has extolled the beauty, and good sense, and rare
accomplishments of Mrs. Howe, the person whom he endeavors to paint
in the most lively and engaging colors, perhaps a little too highly, and

in a style that may appear to those who are acquainted with her to this day romantic and extravagant; and the colonel must needs have been misinformed with respect to some particulars that he has mentioned in her history. Indeed, when I read the extract from his history to Mrs. Tute, (which name she has derived from a third husband, whose widow she now remains,) she seemed to be well pleased, and said at first it was all true, but soon after contradicted the circumstance of her lover's being so bereft of his senses, when he saw her moving off in a boat at some distance from the shore, as to plunge into the water after her, in consequence of which he was seen no more. It is true, she said, that as she was returning from Montreal to Albany, she met with young Saccapee on the way; that she was in a boat with Colonel Schuyler; that the French officer came on board the boat, made her some handsome presents, took his final leave of her, and departed, to outward appearance in tolerable good humor.

She moreover says that when she went to Canada for her daughter, she met with him again; that he showed her a lock of her hair, and her name, likewise, printed with vermilion on his arm. As to her being chosen agent to go to Europe, in behalf of the people of Hinsdale, when Colonel Howard obtained from the government of New York a patent of their lands on the west side of Connecticut River, it was never once thought of by Hinsdale people until the above-mentioned extract arrived among them, in which the author has inserted it as a matter of undoubted fact.

[from Francis Chase, ed., *Gathered Sketches from the Early History of New Hampshire and Vermont* (Claremont, N.H.: Tracy, Kenney & Co., 1856), 75–90.]

Letters Relating to Mrs. Jemima How, Who Was Taken by the Indians at Hinsdale, N.H., in July, 1755

Hinsdale, Jan'y 20th, 1758
To his Excellency, BENNING WENTWORTH, Esq., Capt. Gen. and Commander-in-Chief in and over his Majesty's Province of New-Hampshire, and the honorable his Majesty's Council in said Province

May it please your Excellency and Honors,

I enclose the copy of a letter from Doct. Stukes, and the extract of another covering it, from Col. Whiting, relating to some captives in

Canada taken from these parts. They write to me, I conclude, because I am a neighbor, and one acquainted with their friends and circumstances.

I therefore thought it my duty to lay their case before your Excellency and Honors, for your wise and compassionate consideration. Mrs. How has not estate or relations sufficient for her's and her children's ransom. One of the women taken with her has procured her ransom, and is sent to England, as we hear.

The husband of the other, Mr. Hilkiah Grout, is with me, who has been carefully endeavoring the ransom of his wife and three children ever since their caption, [capture] which was in June, 1755, but as yet can find no method for their relief. He earnestly entreats your favorable aid, direction and assistance herein. We hear Lieut. Johnson had lodged a petition to the General Court relating to the captives, and hope these will come opportunely to be considered therewith, may it be thought proper. If your Excellency and Honors can do or order any thing for their redemption, we should be glad to be informed by Lieut. Parker, the bearer.

I am your Excellency's and Honors most dutiful and obedient servant,

EBENEZER HINSDALE

Letter of Dr. Stukes, referred to in the preceding

NEW-HAVEN, 23d Dec'r, 1757

SR: Having lately come from Canada with Col. Peter Schuyler, we met at Fort St. John's with one Mrs. How, wife of Mr. Caleb How, of your place. She was taken at the time her husband was killed. She has six children with her, and desired me to write to you to let her friends know that she and her children are well, but in miserable circumstances. She is sold to the captain of the Fort St. John's, and is tolerably well used, but her children are sadly used. Her two eldest are to be put into a nunnery. She begs (for God's sake) that you and her friends would do every thing in your power to get her and her children home. She likewise desired me to let you know the women taken with her are very well. I am well assured if you or any of her friends were to know one half of what these poor people suffer, you'd leave no stone unturned to relieve them. I recommend to you the case, not of a man able to go thro' hardships, but of a poor helpless widow, and six fatherless children; which to relieve must be well pleasing in the sight of God.   I am, sir, your very humble servant,

BENJA. STUKES

P.S.—If you please to favor me with a line, direct to B. S., surgeon of the New-Jersey troops in New-York.

Extract of a letter from Col. Whiting to Eben'r Hinsdale

NEW-HAVEN, Dec. 24, 1757

SIR—The enclosed, Dr. Stukes left with me yesterday morning, and desired me to direct and forward it to you. This gentleman came from Canada with Col. Schuyler. I asked him what method could be taken to relieve Mrs. How;—he says Col. Schuyler is to return next spring, as he has given his parole of honor to do, or return some person in exchange. If money could be procured for the ransom of Mrs. How and family, and sent to Col. Schuyler, he will use all endeavors for their ransom.

He is a gentleman of great generosity; and having seen and known the distress of the captives, is disposed to do every thing for their relief, &c. &c.

If you have occasion to write this gentleman, direct to me, and I will take care to forward your letters, &c.

I am your friend and most obedient servant,

N. WHITING

[*Collections of the New Hampshire Historical Society* vol. 5 (Concord: Asa McFarland, 1837), 256–58.]

ZADOCK STEELE

The Connecticut Valley escaped relatively lightly from British and Indian raids during the American Revolution, in part because some Abenakis settled with their families in the Haverhill/Newbury area and served as rangers, helping Colonel Timothy Bedel to protect the settlements against assault. However, in October 1780, Lieutenant Richard Houghton of the British Indian department led some three hundred Indians—mainly Caughnawagas—across Lake Champlain and headed along the Winooski River toward Newbury, where they hoped to capture the American Major Benjamin Whitcomb. When American scouts alerted Newbury, the raiders shifted course, catching by surprise the Vermont villages of Royalton, Randolph, Tunbridge, and Sharon. They burned over two dozen houses, destroyed barns and mills, killed several people and some one hundred fifty head of cattle, and carried off about twenty-seven prisoners and thirty horses.

Though embellished with his own inventions and with scriptural allusions, captive Zadock Steele's account is the most complete record of the attack and the subsequent experiences of the prisoners. This edition varies only slightly in punctuation from that published by the author in Montpelier in 1818 and entitled The Indian Captive; or a Narrative of the Captivity and Sufferings of Zadock Steele. Related by Himself.

[Wes Herwig, "Indian Raid on Royalton," *Vermont Life* (Autumn 1964), 16–21.]

Captivity of Zadock Steele

BEFORE THE mind of the indulgent reader is engaged in a perusal of the sufferings of my maturer years, it may not be improper to direct the attention to scenes of nativity and youth.

The day of my birth, and the events which transpired to bring upon me the miseries I have undergone, will not be uninteresting, I think, to those who may feel disposed to read the following pages.

As, in the evening of a tempestuous day, with solemn yet pleasing emotions we look back on the dangers through which we have been preserved, so, when man has passed through scenes of fatigue, endured the hardships of a savage captivity, as well as the pains of a prison, and again obtained his freedom, it is a source of pleasure to cause those scenes to pass in review before his imagination, and cannot fail to excite his gratitude to the Power that afforded him relief.

I was born at Tolland, Connecticut, on the 17th of December, 1758.

In 1776 my father, James Steele, Esq., moved from Tolland to Ellington, a town adjoining, where he kept a house of entertainment several years. During the years of my childhood the American colonies were put in commotion by what is generally termed the French war.

The colonies had hardly recovered from the convulsions of that war when the American revolution commenced. My father had been actively engaged in the former war, and now received a lieutenant's commission in the revolutionary army. The importance of the contest in which the colonies were engaged called upon every friend to the rights of man to be actively employed. Being in my eighteenth year in May, 1776, I enlisted into the army for one year as waiter to my father. Soon after I enlisted he was visited with a severe fit of sickness, which prevented him from entering the army, and compelled me to go into the ranks, leaving him behind. My two older brothers, Aaron and James, also enlisted the same year. Aaron died in March following at Chatham, New Jersey, in the twenty-third year of his age. Bereft of a brother whom I held dear, after serving the term of my enlistment I returned to Ellington.

The next year I served one campaign in the militia, and the year following as a teamster, which closed my services in the army. I was now about nineteen years of age. I had been favored with very little opportunity, as yet, to acquire an education; as the infantile state of the colonies and the agitation of public affairs at that time afforded little encouragement to schools, and caused a universal depression of literature in general.

I, however, acquired an education sufficient to enable me to transact the business of a farmer and regulate my own concerns in my intercourse with mankind. But long have I deeply regretted the want of that knowledge of letters requisite to prepare for the press a narrative of my own sufferings and those of my fellow-captives which should be read with interest and receive the approbation of an indulgent public.

No hope of pecuniary gain or wish to bring myself into public notice has induced me to publish a narrative of my sufferings. A desire that others as well as myself might learn wisdom from the things I have suffered is the principal cause of its publication. The repeated instances of my deliverance from threatened death, in which the finger of God was visible, call for the deepest gratitude, and have made an impression upon my mind which I trust will remain as long as the powers of my recollection shall endure. I was sensible it might also furnish a lesson of instruction to my fellow-men and to future generations duly to prize the privileges and blessings they may enjoy, by observing the dreadful contrast which is brought to view in this narrative.

Desirable, however, as it might be, I had long since relinquished all idea of ever seeing an account of my sufferings in print. But by the earnest solicitations and friendly though feeble assistance of others, I have thought fit at this late period of my life, yet with humble deference to the good sense of an enlightened public, to give a short narrative of what I have endured in common with many of my fellow-men who were my fellow-prisoners.

Among the evils resulting from the destruction of Royalton, my own captivity was far from being the least. That event was the precursor of all my sorrows—the fountain from which sprung streams of wretchedness and want. Nor will the channel be forgotten, though the raging flood cease to roll. As small streams are swallowed up by larger ones, so many serious and sore trials are doubtless lost in that dreadful current of distress through which I was called to pass.

The attention of the reader is, however, requested to a simple statement of facts, as they occur to my mind, while I relate the circumstances of my captivity by the Indians, the treatment I received from them, my privations while a prisoner to the British, my wonderful escape from their hands, and extreme sufferings in the wilderness on my way home. Truth will not easily permit, nor have I any desire, to enlarge or exaggerate upon the things I suffered. Guided by the principles of justice, and wishing no ill to any man or set of men, I hope I shall not be found disposed to calumniate or reproach.

It is not my intention to speak of any individual or nation with less respect than is due to their true character and conduct.

I shall, however, be under the necessity of noticing many cruelties that were inflicted upon the prisoners, by men who enjoyed the advantages of civilization, which were sufficient to put the rudest savage to the blush.

But the long lapse of time and the effects of old age have, no doubt, blotted from my memory incidents which would have been no less, and perhaps more, interesting and instructive than many circumstances which I shall be able to recollect. This, together with the inexperience of the writer, must be the only apology for the imperfections of the following pages.

In April, 1780, being in my twenty-second year, I started from my father's house in Ellington, leaving all my friends and relatives, and came to Randolph, in the State of Vermont, a town south of Brookfield, a distance of nearly two hundred miles. I there purchased a right of land, lying in the north part of the town, on which was a log house and a little improvement. Suffering the privations and hardships common to those who dwell in new countries, I spent the summer in diligent labor, sub-sisting upon rather coarse fare, and supported by the fond hopes of soon experiencing better days.

The young man who drove my team from Connecticut, with provi-sions, farming utensils, &c., labored with me through the summer and fall seasons till October, when he returned to Ellington just in time to escape the danger of being taken by the Indians.

A small settlement had commenced in the south-westerly part of Ran-dolph, on the third branch of White River, about six miles from my own. A little settlement had also commenced on the second branch of the same river in Brookfield, in the easterly part of the town, and at about an equal distance from my abode. As there were in Randolph a number of families situated in different parts of the town, and our country being engaged in a war, which rendered our frontier settlements exposed to the ravages of an exasperated foe, we had taken the necessary precaution to establish alarm posts, by which we might announce to each other the approach of an enemy.

But our Brookfield brethren, though in a town adjoining, were be-yond the hearing of the report of our alarm guns.

On the 16th of October we were apprised of the arrival of the Indians at Royalton, a town about ten miles south of Randolph. They entered that town on the morning of the 16th, and were committing ravages, taking and killing the inhabitants, sparing the lives of none whom they could overtake in an attempt to escape, destroying property, burning all the buildings that they discovered, killing the cattle, pillaging the houses, and taking captives.

It was expected they would follow up either the second or third branch on their return to Canada, as these two branches run to the south and nearly parallel to each other; the former of which empties itself into the river at Royalton, and the latter a few miles west.

I was employed during the sixteenth day till nearly night in assisting the settlers on the third branch in Randolph to move their families and effects into the woods such a distance as was thought would render them safe, should the Indians pursue that stream up on their return.

I then requested that some one of them should accompany me to go and notify the Brookfield settlers of their danger. Being unable to per-suade any to go with me, I started alone. I had only time to arrive at my own dwelling, which was on my direct course, before I was overtaken by the approach of night. As there was no road and nothing but marked trees to guide my way, I tarried all night. Having prepared some food for breakfast I lay down to sleep, little knowing what awaited my waking hours. At the dawn of day on the morning of the 17th I set out to prosecute the object for which I started, though in a violent tempest, attended with snow. I had not proceeded far before the storm greatly increased, which I found would not only much endanger my life, but so retard my progress that I could not arrive in time seasonably to warn my friends of their danger or escape myself from the hands of the enemy should they follow the second branch instead of the third. I therefore returned to my house. Soon after I arrived within doors, filled with anxiety for the unsuspecting inhabitants of Brookfield, I heard a shocking cry in the surrounding woods; and, trembling for my own safety, I ran to the door, when, to my utter astonishment, and the reader may judge my feelings, I beheld a company of Indians, consisting of not less than three hundred in number, not ten rods distant, approaching with hideous cries and frightful yells!

"O how unlike the chorus of the skies!"

There was no way of escape. I had only to stand still, wait their approach, and receive my miserable destiny. Indeed, I could now say with David, "The sorrows of death compassed me, and the floods of ungodly men made me afraid." I had nowhere to flee but the "great Preserver of men, who was my only hiding-place," "my goodness and my fortress, my high tower and my deliverer, my shield, and he in whom I trust."

"They came upon me as a wide breaking of waters; in the desolation they rolled themselves upon me."

Their leader came up and told me I must go with them. They asked me if any other persons were to be found near that place. I told them it was probable there were none to be found. They then inquired if any cattle were near; to which I answered in the negative. But they seemed to choose rather to take the trouble to search than to confide in what I told them.

After taking every thing they found worthy to carry with them, and destroying all that was not likely to suffer injury by fire, they set the house on fire and marched on. One of them took a bag of grass seed upon his back, and, cutting a hole in the bag, scattered the seed as he marched, which took root, stocked the ground, and was for many years a sad memento of my long captivity.

The chief who came up to me could talk English very well, which was a circumstance much in my favor, as he became my master, under which name I shall have frequent occasion to speak of him in the course of this narrative.

They took all my clothes, not excepting the best I had on, and distributed them amongst themselves. They, however, furnished me with blankets sufficient to defend me against the cold, but deprived me of my own property; the bitter consequences of which I felt in my subsequent confinement with the British, and on my return to resume my settlement at Randolph.

The Indians had encamped the night preceding on the second branch in Randolph, on which the Brookfield settlers lived, and not more than ten miles below them, but during the night had been put to rout by a party of Americans, consisting of about two hundred and fifty in number, who were commanded by Colonel John House, of Hanover, New Hampshire. To make their escape, they left the stream and took a course which brought them directly to my dwelling.

Had they not been molested, but permitted to pursue their intended course up the stream, the defenceless inhabitants of Brookfield would doubtless have shared the miserable fate of the inhabitants of Royalton, themselves taken prisoners, and doomed to suffer a long and wretched captivity, and their property destroyed by the devouring element. This prevention, which, however, was the cause of my captivity, the subject of the following narrative, was probably the only good that Colonel H. effected; and this he did unwittingly, for which he can claim no thanks.

Soon after we started from my house my master, who was the principal conductor and chief of the whole tribe, discovered that I had a pair of silver buckles in my shoes, and attempted to take them from me; but, by promising to let him have them when we arrived at our journey's end, I persuaded him to let me keep them. But we had not travelled far before another Indian espied them, and crying out, *"Wah stondorum!"* (Ah, there's silver!) took them from me, and furnished me with strings for my shoes as substitutes.

We travelled the first day to Berlin and encamped on Dog River, not many miles from the place where Montpelier village now stands. They built a fire of some rods in length, to which opportunity was afforded for all to approach. They then placed sentinels around, which rendered it impossible for any one to move unnoticed. But this precaution was not sufficient to satisfy their minds to prevent the escape of their captive prisoners. Therefore, to render our escape less easy to be effected, as we lay down upon the ground they tied a rope around our bodies, and, extending it each way, the Indians laid upon it on our right and on our left, not suffering any two prisoners to lie next each other. I could, however, crawl so far out of the rope as to be able to sit upright, but always found some of the Indians sitting up, either to prepare their clothing for the following day's march, or intentionally to set as additional guards; and I never found the favored moment when all were at rest.

As they had told me before we encamped that if they were overtaken by the Americans they should kill every prisoner, I felt the more anxious to make my escape; and they seemed, in view of their danger, more desirous to keep us within reach of the tomahawk, and secure us against a flight in case the Americans should approach. I watched with trembling fear and anxious expectation during the night we lay at Berlin, seeking an opportunity to escape, which I found utterly impossible, and looking every moment for the arrival of a company of Americans, whose approach I was assured would be attended with death to every prisoner.

They compelled many of the prisoners to carry their packs, enormous in size and extremely heavy, as they were filled with the plunder of pillaged houses and every thing which attracted their curiosity or desire to possess. Looking glasses, which by the intention or carelessness of the prisoners became broken in a short time, pots, spiders, frying pans, and old side saddles, which were sold on their arrival at St. John's for one dollar, composed a part of their invaluable baggage.

On the morning of the 18th they first ordered me to eat my breakfast, urging me to eat as much as I wanted; while, on account of the loss of their provisions at Randolph, they had scarce half an allowance for themselves. I knew not whether to attribute this conduct to their feelings of charity and generosity, a desire to secure my friendship, or a wish to preserve my life under a prospect of procuring gain, or to some other cause.

Indeed, they seemed at all times to be willing to "feed the hungry," not even seeing one of the prisoners leisurely pick a berry by the way, as they passed along, without offering them food, considering this as a token of our hunger.

Their food, however, was very unsavory, insomuch that nothing but extreme hunger would have induced me to eat of it, though I always had a share of their best.

Habituated to a partial covering themselves and excited by curiosity, they took from me all my best clothes, and gave me blankets in exchange. They often travelled with the utmost celerity in their power to try my activity, viewing me with looks of complacency to find me able to keep pace with them.

We this day passed down Dog River till we came to Onion River, into which the former empties itself, and then kept the course of the latter during the day, steering nearly a north-west direction. At night we came to a very steep mountain, which was extremely difficult of access, not far from the place now called Bolton, in the county of Chittenden. Upon the top of this mountain the Indians, on their way to Royalton, had secreted a number of bags of fine flour which they brought with them from Canada, and now regained. This greatly replenished their stores, and afforded a full supply of wholesome bread. The manner of making their bread is curious, and exhibits useful instruction to those who may be called to make their bread in the wilderness without enjoying the privilege of household furniture.

They took their dough, wound it around a stick in the form of a screw, stuck it into the ground by the fire, and thus baked their bread, without receiving injury by the smoke or rendering it more filthy than it came from their hands.

Their fear that they should be overtaken by the Americans had by this time greatly abated, and this was considered by the prisoners grounds for less apprehension of the danger of being put to death by the Indians. Till now, however, it is beyond the power of language to express, nor can imagination paint, the feelings of my heart, when, torn from my friends and all I held dear on earth, compelled to roam the wilderness to unknown parts, obliged to ford rivers, and then lie down at night upon the cold ground with scarcely a dry thread in my clothes, having a rope fastened around my body, surrounded by a tribe of savage Indians, from whose very friendship I could expect nothing but wretchedness and misery, and whose brutal rage would be sure to prove my death.

Nor was this rage only liable to be excited by a sense of real danger, but, from conscious guilt, equally liable to be put in force by the most slight, false, and trifling alarm.

> "'Tis a prime part of happiness to know
> How much unhappiness must prove our lot—
> A part which few possess."

On the fourth day we arrived at Lake Champlain. We here found some bateaux, in which the Indians had conveyed themselves thither on their way to Royalton. On their arrival at the lake, and regaining their bateaux, they gave a shout of exultation and laughter, manifesting their joy and triumph.

My master, who was about to take a different route from the rest of the tribe, took me aside, and, in a dissembling tone, told me with great professions of friendship, with little credit, however, that I had better take off my coat and let him have it, for which he would give me a blanket in exchange, assuring me that the Indians would take it from me if I did not do it. Dreading the consequences of a refusal more than the loss of the coat, I let him have it, and received a blanket in return. We crossed over and encamped on Grand Isle that night. The next morning we reëmbarked in our bateaux, and safely landed at the Isle Aux Noix before night. Here the Indians found a supply of rum, which gave them an opportunity to make market for a part of their plunder and satiate their thirst. Nor, indeed, was the opportunity unimproved. Irritated by the force of intoxication, they were all in confusion: savage yells and shrill outcries filled the surrounding atmosphere, and death seemed to stare every captive full in the face.

> "So sung Philander, as a friend went round
> In the rich ichor, in the generous blood
> Of Bacchus, purple god of joyous wit."

At length, however, their senses became drowned in the torrent of inebriety; they sank into a helpless state, and reposed in the arms of insensibility. As we had now arrived within the dominions of the British, and were not only guarded by a number of the Indians who were not under the power of intoxication, but watched by the enemy's subjects resident at that place, we could find no opportunity to make our escape.

The next morning, which was the sixth day of our march, we started for St. John's, and arrived there that day. At this place, likewise, the Indians found a plenty of ardent spirits, by a too free use of which they became more enraged, if possible, than before.

They now began to threaten the lives of all the captives whose faces were not painted, as the face being painted was a distinguishing mark put upon those whom they designed not to kill.

As I was not painted, one of the Indians, under the influence of intoxication and brutal rage, like many white people, more sagacious than humane, came up to me, and, pointing a gun directly at my head, cocked it, and was about to fire, when an old Indian, who was my new master, knocked it aside, pushed him backwards upon the ground, and took a bottle of rum, and, putting it to his mouth, turned down his throat a considerable quantity, left him, and went on.

The punishment seemed in no way to displease the criminal: he wished he would continue to punish him through the day in the same manner; regarding the momentary gratification of appetite more than all other blessings of life, or even life itself.

They now procured some paint and painted my face, which greatly appeased the rage of those who, before, had been apparently determined to take my life. I now received their marks of friendship, nor felt myself in danger of becoming the subject of their fatal enmity. Clothed with an Indian blanket, with my hands and my face painted, and possessing activity equal to any of them, they appeared to be willing I should live with them and be accounted as one of their number.

We arrived at Caghnewaga on the seventh day of our march. Thus I found myself, within the space of seven days, removed from my home and from all my relatives the distance of about three hundred miles, almost destitute of clothing, entirely without money, with no other associates than a race of savage Indians, whose language I could not understand, whose diet was unsavory and unwholesome, whose "tender mercies are cruel," barbarism their civility, no pardon to an enemy their established creed, and presented with no other prospect for the future than a captivity for life, a final separation from all earthly friends, and situated in an enemy's country.

In short, stripped of every comfort that sweetens life except the "one thing needful, which the world can neither give nor take away," my temporal prospects were banished and lost forever. No earthly friends to administer consolation or with whom to sympathize, nor hope of escape to feed upon, truly, humble submission to the will of Heaven, and an entire "trust in the Lord," was the only balm afforded me.

> "A soul prepared for such a state as this
> Is heir expectant to immortal bliss."

Some days after we arrived at Caghnewaga, an old man by the name of Philips, whose silver locks bespoke the experience of many winters; whose visage indicated the trials, sorrows, and afflictions of a long and wretched captivity; whose wrinkled face and withered hands witnessed the sufferings of many hardships, and presented to me a solemn and awful token of what I myself might expect to suffer,—came and told me that I was about to be adopted into one of the Indian families, to fill the place of one whom they had lost on their expedition to Royalton.

Mr. Philips was taken prisoner in the western part of the State of New York, by the Indians, in his youthful days, and, having been adopted into one of their families, had always lived with them. He had retained his knowledge of the English language, and served as an interpreter for the tribe.

The ceremony of my own adoption, as well as that of many other of the prisoners, afforded no small degree of diversion. The scene presented to view a spectacle of an assemblage of barbarism assuming the appearance of civilization.

All the Indians, both male and female, together with the prisoners, assembled and formed a circle, within which one of their chiefs, standing upon a stage erected for the purpose, harangued the audience in the Indian tongue. Although I could not understand his language, yet I could plainly discover a great share of native eloquence. His speech was of considerable length, and its effect obviously manifested weight of argument, solemnity of thought, and at least human sensibility. I was placed near by his side, and had a fair view of the whole circle. After he had ended his speech an old squaw came and took me by the hand and led me to her wigwam, where she dressed me in a red coat, with a ruffle in my bosom, and ordered me to call her mother. She could speak English tolerably well; but was very poor, and therefore unable to furnish me with very sumptuous fare. My food was rather beneath a savage mediocrity; though no doubt my new mother endeavored as far as lay in her power to endear the affections of her newly-adopted yet ill-natured son.

I found the appellation of *mother* highly pleased the tawny jade, which proportionably increased my disgust, already intolerable; and, instead of producing contentment of mind, added disquietude to affliction and sorrow.

As I was blessed with an excellent voice for singing, I was the more beloved by, and, on that account, received much better treatment from, my new mother, as well as from other Indians.

I was allowed the privilege of visiting any part of the village in the daytime, and was received with marks of fraternal affection and treated with all the civility an Indian is capable to bestow.

A prisoner, by the name of Belknap, was set about hewing some poles for a stable door while his Indian master held them for him. As he hewed, the Indian, sitting upon the pole, suffered it gradually to turn over, though unperceived by him; which occasioned the workman, who saw its operation, laughing in his sleeves, to hew quite round the stick, in hewing from end to end. Thinking that Belknap knew no better, the Indian endeavored to instruct him. After trying several poles with the same success, the Indian, filled with impatience for this untractable pupil, with his eyes on fire, left him and called his interpreter to make his wishes more distinctly known; to whom Belknap declared, that he did well understand the wishes of the Indian, and was determined to avoid doing his will.

After remaining in this condition a few weeks, finding the prisoners very incorrigible, and wishing for the reward they might obtain for them, information was given the prisoners that they might be delivered over to the British at Montreal as prisoners of war, or continue with the Indians, as they should choose.

We sought the advice of an English gentleman, by the name of Stacy, resident in the village of Caghnewaga, who had married a squaw for his wife, and was extensively acquainted, not only with the affairs of the Indians, but with the citizens of Montreal. He appeared to be a man of integrity and veracity, was employed in merchandise, and also served as one of their interpreters.

I was advised by Mr. Stacy to be delivered into the hands of the British. He said I might doubtless obtain leave to dwell in some family of a private gentleman until I should be exchanged.

Encouraged by the prospect of enjoying the company of civilized people, and flattered with the idea of being soon exchanged, and thereby enabled to return once more to see my friends in Connecticut, I made choice to be given up to the British. All the captives did likewise.

We were all conducted to Montreal, by the Indians, in the latter part of November, 1780, and there "sold for a half joe" each. Most of the captives were young, and remarkably robust, healthy, and vigorous. I was now almost twenty-two years of age. To be compelled to spend the vigor of my days in useless confinement was a source of grief and pain to my mind; but I could see no way of escape. The wisdom of God I found to be unsearchable indeed. I felt, however, a good degree of submission to the providence of the Most High, and a willingness to "accept of the punishment of mine iniquities."

We found at the city of Montreal about one hundred and seventy prisoners, some of whom were made captives by the Indians in different parts of America, and others had been taken prisoners of war in forts by capitulation and by conquest. Here we could see women and children, who had fallen the victims of savage captivity, weeping and mourning their fate, whose tears, trickling down their cheeks, bespoke the language of their hearts. It was enough to melt the heart of stone with grief to behold the bosoms of the "poor widows" heaving with sighs and to hear their groans; while the companions of their youth, their bosom friends and partners in life, were no more, having spilled their blood and laid down their lives in defence of their country, their families, and their firesides.

Here I beheld the orphan, fatherless and motherless, whose tender age called for compassion and required the kind protection of an affectionate mother, whose infantile mind rendered it incapable of telling its name, the place of its birth, or giving any information respecting itself or its parents.

This led me to consider my own sufferings comparatively small; and a sense of my own wretched condition became lost in the feelings of compassion for these unhappy widows and orphans.

We were put into a large building, called the Old Regal Church, with the other prisoners, in which we were kept several days, when we were removed into a large stone building, fitted up for the purpose, in the suburbs of the city, upon the shore of the River St. Lawrence.

I often made application for liberty to take quarters in the family of some private gentleman, where I might enjoy the advantages of a common slave until I should be able to procure a ransom or be exchanged, urging the manner of my being taken and my destitute situation as arguments in my favor, having been stripped of all my property by the Indians and deprived of all my change of clothes. But all my efforts proved only a witness to myself and my fellow-sufferers of that deafness to the calls of humanity which is always the characteristic of tyranny and despotism.

Many of the prisoners as well as myself had only one shirt, and were obliged to go without any while we washed that. Indolence and disregard for cleanliness prevented many from doing this, which may be reckoned among the many causes that brought our subsequent evils upon us. We were allowed, or rather said to be allowed, one pound of bread and one pound of fresh beef per day. But, through the injustice and dishonesty of the person who dealt out our allowance, we were robbed even of a part of this humble pittance. Had we been able to obtain our full allowance in provisions of good quality, we should have been able to have furnished ourselves with other necessary articles; but now we were deprived of the privilege by the curtailment of our rations. We were obliged by the calls of hunger to pound up the beef bones, which composed no small share of our rations of meat, and boil them for broth. We had no butter, cheese, flour, nor any kind of sauce during the winter. We were kept almost totally without firewood, having scarcely enough to enable us to cook our meat. Our beds consisted principally of blankets, which they brought from the hospital in all their filth. This was an apparent manifestation of their disregard at least for the prisoners, if not a malevolent design to introduce that contagion which should spread disease, desolation, and death throughout our camp.

Pinched with hunger, half naked, and chilled with the cold, we were forced to have recourse to our beds, and occupy them a great part of the time, though they were the habitations of filthy vermin, tainted with the infections of mortal distempers, and scented with the nauseous smell of the dying and the dead.

The complicated collection of people of different habits, comprising almost every kind of foul and vicious character, and the combination of so many events, either of which should seem alone sufficient to create disease, caused a general and universal prevalence of the itch.

Our close confinement was, to some of the prisoners, a source of grief; to others a cloak of indulgence in laziness; while to all it was the mother of disease, the harbinger of pain.

We suffered so much with hunger that we should have thankfully "fed upon the crums that fell from the rich man's table;" and so great were our afflictions that we should have gladly caressed the "dog that had come and licked our sores."

While I was a captive with the Indians I was in sorrow, and "desired a better country." And I had not experienced the "trial of cruel mockings and scourgings, of bonds and imprisonment," sufficiently to enable me to say with Paul, "I have learned in whatsoever state I am therewith to be content." When we were put into the hands of the British "we looked for peace, but no good came; and for a time of health, and beheld trouble." Indeed, it may justly be said of them, "They turned the needy out of the way; they caused the naked to lodge without clothing, that they have no covering in the cold; they pluck the fatherless from the breast, and take a pledge of the poor; they cause him to go naked without clothing, and they take away the sheaf from the hungry." (Job xxiv. 4–7, 10.) I pleaded that they would "make me as one of their hired servants;" but they would not.

In the spring, after being "brought low, through oppression, affliction, and sorrow," we were supplied with salt pork, bread, oatmeal, and peas in abundance. As we had long been almost starved, our avidity for the food which was now before us may more easily be imagined than described. Let it suffice us to say, that none ate sparingly, but all greedily. Indeed, some seemed not only anxious to satisfy hunger, but determined to revenge for their past sufferings. This sudden repletion of our wants produced the scurvy among the prisoners, which threatened death to every one. Reiterated sighs and dying groans now filled our camp.

To such an alarming degree did this dreadful disease prevail that many were obliged to be removed to the hospital for relief; distress and anguish pervaded the whole body of the prisoners; and the citizens of Montreal, alarmed, perhaps, for their own safety, seemed to feel anxious for our relief. But justice requires I should state that we received at this time all that kind attention which was due to our wretched condition and every favor in the power of our keepers to bestow; while the inhabitants manifested a humane disposition, and displayed the generous feelings of pity and tender compassion. In short, conscious that they, in truth, had all partially contributed to increase our miseries, they seemed to feel a relenting for their past misconduct, which excited them to use their utmost exertion to exonerate themselves from guilt by their subsequent good offices for our relief.

They furnished us with green herbs and every thing which was adapted to our disorders or calculated for our comfort and recovery. By these means our health was fully restored, gratitude and joy sat smiling on every countenance, and songs of deliverance dwelt on every tongue. Pain now gave place to pleasure, sorrow fled as happiness approached, murmurs and complaints which had long been the universal cry now were heard no more, and quietude was felt in every breast.

After our recovery we were allowed the privilege of a yard, of some rods square in extent, by which we were enabled to exercise for the preservation of our health. But at length some of the prisoners made their escape, which occasioned all the rest to be put into close confinement and kept under lock and key. We were supplied, however, with all the comforts of life, so far as our close confinement would permit.

In October, 1781, all the prisoners were removed to an island in the River St. Lawrence, called Prison Island, about forty-five miles above the city of Montreal, and opposite to a place called Cateau du Lac. Here we were furnished with a full supply of wholesome food during our confinement on the island.

This island is situated a little below the Lake St. Francis, which is formed by a large swell in the River St. Lawrence, and was considered a very eligible place for the confinement of the prisoners. Indeed, it was thought impossible that any person destitute of boats should be able to escape without being drowned, as the water ran with the utmost velocity on each side of the island. We were, therefore, allowed the liberty of traversing the whole island, which contained about twenty acres.

Guarded by a company of refugees and tories possessing as little humanity as patriotism, and having long been the miserable sufferers of a wretched captivity and painful imprisonment, many of the prisoners attempted to make their escape by swimming down the current the distance of three miles. But few succeeded, while some were drowned in the hazardous attempt. The captain of the guard, whose name was M'Daniel, was a tory, and as totally devoid of humanity and generosity as the Arab who traverses the deserts of Africa. His conduct towards the prisoners was such as ought to stamp his character with infamy and disgrace. Cruelty to the prisoners seemed to be his greatest delight. I once saw one of the prisoners plunge into the river in the daytime and swim down the current the distance of three miles, but was discovered by M'Daniel soon after he started, who ordered him to be shot before he should ever reach shore; but a British soldier, possessing more humanity than his commander, waded into the river and took hold of the trembling prisoner, almost exhausted, declaring, "if the prisoner was shot, he would be likewise."

The malignant disposition of M'Daniel and the invidious character of the guard induced the prisoners to seek opportunity and confront almost every danger to effect their escape. But time soon rolled away, till winter approached, without bringing to our view that propitious moment which could afford the slightest hope of success in the attempt. On the one hand, the eye of an implacable foe was upon us, with rancor, malice, and revenge in his bosom, and the implements of destruction in his hand; and on the other, the rapid current of the stream threatened us with death if we approached; while the foaming billows, roaring in a voice like thunder, bade us beware.

Desperate, indeed, must be the attempt for any one knowingly to plunge himself into the jaws of death to escape from trouble.

At the approach of winter, the ice below the island rendered it visibly and utterly impossible to escape alive. We were, therefore, now forced into submission, and had only to consult together upon those measures which should be most likely to promote our own happiness while we waited the return of spring.

In January we were ordered by M'Daniel to shovel the snow for a path, in which the guard were to travel while on their duty.

Regarding the proverb of Solomon as worthy of our notice, that "it is an honor for a man to cease from strife," we complied with the demand, thus sacrificing our rights on the altar of peace. But now, finding by ocular demonstration the verity of a like proverb of the same wise man, that "every fool will be meddling," we unanimously agreed to disobey all similar orders and every command which should be afterwards given contrary to right. We were not insensible that the prisoner, though unable to defend, was possessed of certain inalienable rights, which we resolved to assert, and refuse obedience to the tyrant who should attempt to encroach upon them. The time soon arrived when duty called us boldly to assert our rights, and manly firmness forbade submission.

We were again commanded by M'Daniel to shovel the snow, to make a path for the guard to travel in; while they themselves had nothing to do but to wait our toil. Disdaining to become slaves, we had universally determined to reject their unauthorized servitude. I therefore informed the infamous M'Daniel what was our unanimous resolution, and told him I feared less what he should dare to do than I did the consequences of yielding to the lawless requisitions of a petty tyrant. Enraged at the opposition of the prisoners to his arbitrary commands, and more highly exasperated against me as the organ, he directed me to be put in irons and carried to the guard house. After uttering the most dreadful threats and horrid imprecations, and finding I was not easily terrified nor readily forced to abandon my rights, he carried his order into execution, took me to the guard house, put me in irons, and kept me there during the whole day till night, when he came and repeated his threats of torture and death in case I continued to refuse compliance. But still finding me unmoved in my determination, and that "hatred stirreth up strifes," he ordered me to be kept in irons till nine o'clock at night without food and then sent back to my barrack.

This was accordingly done, though some Dutchmen, terrified at my fate, consented to his requirements and performed the service while I was confined in the guard house. In consequence of our refusal to comply with his unjust and illegal demands, the most severe punishments and barbarous cruelties were inflicted upon the prisoners.

"To revenge upon," he said, "no prisoner should be allowed to have a fire another night while they remained on the island."

Accordingly the guard came into our barracks every night with large quantities of snow and put out all the fires, using as much caution not to leave a spark unquenched as though the lives of thousands and the wealth of a metropolis were at stake.

"Though seen, we labor to believe it true."

What malice is manifest in the breasts of those who labor with diligence and toil with pain to increase the misery of those who are already wretched and groaning in sorrow!

Here we beheld the depravity of man. Here we could see the fulfilment of that passage of holy writ which declares that, "because sentence against an evil work is not executed speedily, therefore the heart of the sons of men is fully set in them to do evil."

Here we could behold a full display of the seven abominations in the sight of God: "A proud look, a lying tongue, and hands that shed innocent blood, a heart that deviseth wicked imaginations, feet that be swift in running to mischief, a false witness that speaketh lies, and him that soweth discord among brethren." (Prov. vi. 16, &c.)

Here we could see monsters in human shape feeding upon revenge; for the labor which they unjustly required of us was not a tenth part of what they performed every night by putting out our fires to punish us for non-compliance with their tyrannical demands. But, possessing the spirit of freemen, we "chose rather to suffer affliction" than to become the slaves of a set of despicable refugees and tories, feeling assured that our affliction would afford us more consolation in the hour of reflection than could be found in a servitude imposed upon us by an infamous renegade.

As our barracks were very cold and open, and being scantily clothed, we suffered greatly for want of fire, to support which we were willing to get wood ourselves. But our keepers chose rather to suffer pain themselves than to permit us to enjoy comfort.

M'Daniel, however, was called away, and succeeded by one M'Kelpin in command. He was also a refugee, the son of a tory, and had the appearance of a raw boy not more than eighteen or nineteen years old, whose very visage portended evil and bade the prisoners prepare for trouble.

His father, he said, had received very ill treatment from the American army, and he had also shared with his father in the abuse for not engaging in the rebellion against the British government. As "the rod is for the back of him that is void of understanding," we doubted not the truth of his statement, nor felt disposed to question but that he received very severe treatment, and more especially when the station in which he was found was taken into consideration; for this, together with the littleness of his mind and the malignity of his temper, will forever prove his want of patriotism and stamp his indignant character with infamy and disgrace as long as evil shall be had in remembrance.

His immature age can be no palliation of his crimes, nor admit of much hope of his reformation by repentance; for, like all other fools, "he hated knowledge, and was wise in his own conceit." Inheriting from his father all the qualities of a knave, and the cowardice of a western savage, who looks for security from danger in his own flight only or in the strength of his allies, he perverted the power put into his hands to do good; used it as a weapon of revenge and an instrument of cruelty. His paternal education was, at the best, toryism, perfectly congenial to his natural disposition. In short, "he was wise to do evil; but to do good he had no knowledge." His first steps towards tyranny and oppression met no opposition; as we wished to enjoy peace, and were willing to yield a portion of our rights to the enjoyment of so invaluable a blessing. But our indulgence served only to stimulate him in the course of revengeful tyranny; and he seemed the more angry, as if "coals of fire were heaped upon his head."

Manifesting a desire to meet with opposition, by using every exertion to provoke to rage, he ordered the prisoners to shovel the snow from the door of his own house. As the prisoners discovered in him a settled determination to pursue compliance with greater and more grievous burdens until he could meet a refusal to comply, we resolved to reject all further encroachments upon our rights. We therefore refused to obey his arbitrary commands any longer. As there was a fort directly opposite the island where a company of soldiers were stationed, we feared the consequences of a revolt, and could only refuse our obedience without making any actual resistance. The prisoner to whom he addressed himself possessed courage equal to the most trying scene, and, choosing rather to suffer an honorable death in defence of his rights than to endure an ignominious life of captive slavery, he met the infamous M'Kelpin with firmness and intrepidity, although he had no prospects of any thing but to endure extreme torture, if not death itself. And this he was the more inclined to do, since it was the avowed object of the infamous villain "to wreak his vengeance upon the unhappy prisoners for injuries," which he said he had received from men who were entire strangers to us, and in which abuse he well knew we took no agency or even had any knowledge.

When the prisoner refused compliance, M'Kelpin came up with a bayonet pointing directly at him, and thrust it within a few inches of his breast, threatening to run him through the heart if he did not immediately comply. But the prisoner, continuing firm in his obstinacy, replied with dauntless courage and deliberate coolness, "Run me through if you dare; I fear you not." Enraged at this reply, M'Kelpin repeated his threats with redoubled vehemence and infuriated madness, and again rushed at the prisoner with the greatest violence, thus endeavoring to terrify him into submission to his will. But the prisoner, with all the appearance of a full sense of death and supported by the rectitude of his motives, met M'Kelpin with manly firmness and true heroism, putting his hand upon his breast, and telling the impertinent fugitive that "he had resolved to die before he should yield obedience to the arbitrary commands of one whose name was synonymous with disgrace, and whose very visage bespoke the corruptions of a heart loaded with every thing that is requisite to fit a soul to become an inhabitant of the regions of blackness and darkness forever." After repeating his threats and menaces several times, and each time receiving the most unqualified denials from the prisoner, he proceeded to punish all such as refused compliance with his request. He associated with threats the most daring oaths and awful imprecations, as if he would endeavor to establish his own authority by manifesting to the world his want of the fear of God and a disregard of every thing that is good.

Like many of the present day, he appeared to imagine that he should be thought to possess uncommon courage and power unlimited if he dared, openly and without fear, to blaspheme the name of Him who is the Ruler of all people, of every language, tongue, and nation. Finding all his threatenings in vain, and discovering that no one would yield obedience to his requirements, forgetting or disregarding the injustice of his claim, and lost in the torrent of anger and revenge, he came, with a guard of soldiers possessing feelings in perfect coincidence with his own, and took the defenceless yet dauntless prisoner whom he had threatened to run through with his bayonet, conveyed him to the barrack, which was used for an ash house, put him in irons, and left him to suffer in the cold the malicious gratification of his malignant and revengeful disposition; telling the innocent and unfortunate victim of his relentless fury that "he was glad he refused to comply with his demands, because he had long wanted and had anxiously sought opportunity to wreak his vengeance on him, and gave the order to shovel the snow from his own door for no other purpose but to excite the opposition of the prisoners, and thus find occasion to punish them, and at the same time take revenge on them for the abuse he had received from the Americans." He then proceeded to order others to shovel the snow; and, being still refused compliance, he threatened and confined in the same manner as he did the first, until he had collected together and confined in that cold barrack the number of twenty-one, who were all handcuffed and chained to the posts of the barrack. This was in January, 1782, when the cold was exceeding severe, and hardly permitted a comfortable seat by the fireside, or admitted of a lodging free from suffering in our closed barracks with a large quantity of blankets.

Here they were ordered to be kept in this barrack, with the windows and doors open to the wind and snow, all that day and the next night. But most of them made their escape to their own barracks before the next morning, some with frozen hands and feet, others with their ears and faces frozen; and, indeed, all having some part of their bodies frozen, and bearing the miserable tokens of their wretched sufferings.

But their escape, notwithstanding the visible and abiding marks of their pain and distress, only exasperated the mind of the unfeeling M'Kelpin, and so enraged the desperate villain that he the next day morning selected the same prisoners, and, with a heart harder than adamant and hands more cruel than the grave, again confined them all in irons and ordered them to be put into the chamber of one of the barracks, there to be kept during that day, the next night, and the following day, without provision, any food, or even a quid of tobacco.

Destitute of any clothing except their wearing apparel, which was poor; confined in irons, in a small, cold room; having no food of any kind; deprived of a luxury which habit had rendered necessary to preserve health; and groaning under the severe pains of their frozen bodies,—their sufferings cannot easily be imagined, far less described.

It was my happy lot, however, not to fall into this number of miserable sufferers of human depravity who were put into the ash house and in the chamber. But the sufferings which I have mentioned were only a prelude to more painful torments and greater barbarities. They were taken from the barrack chamber one by one, carried to the guard house, and tortured in the most cruel manner. Some were surrounded with soldiers, armed with guns and bayonets pointing directly at them, and so near as to render the prisoners unable to move without being pierced with the bayonets; while the infamous M'Kelpin whipped the prisoners and caned them till he had glutted his vengeance. Who can describe the inhuman scene? To see a prisoner, the victim of cruelty and wretchedness, guiltless and defenceless, confined in irons with his hands behind him, ready to faint for want of food, groaning under the excruciating pains of his frozen limbs, bathed in blood which gushed from his mangled body, tears flowing from his eyes in streams, which bespoke in language more forcible than a voice like thunder, as they trickled down his frozen cheeks, the sorrows of a heart swollen with grief and racked with pain. I could say with Job, "Mine eye is also dim by reason of sorrow, and all my members are as a shadow."

Others of this unhappy number were hung up by the neck till nearly dead, while their hands were confined in irons and their faces black with death, when they were taken down, and the irons which had bound their hands jammed into their mouths till they were filled with blood. Who could behold this and not weep and mourn for the depravity of man left to himself? Who can witness a scene like this without acknowledging with self-application the truth of those words which fell from our Savior's lips to the unbelieving Jews, "Ye are of your father the devil, and the lusts of your father ye will do"? After enduring these horrid barbarities and inhuman tortures, inflicted by men professing the principles of humanity, the unhappy sufferers were sent back to their barracks, there to weep and bewail their miserable fate. Often have my cheeks been wet with tears of commiseration, while my heart ached within me, for these unfortunate sufferers of the unrestrained vengeance of a depraved villain. Nor was I left to be reminded of their torture and distress only by a recollection of the past; but my eyes could witness the scars of wounds and behold the palefaced visage of death abiding on the countenance of many, which were received by the cruelties of this horrid scene. And, alas! I needed only to look at myself and all around me to remind me of the woeful case of those whose lot it is to fall into the hands and become the victims of a revengeful tyrant, and suffer the wrath of a man totally devoid of mercy, unrestrained either by the authority of a superior, the laws of his country, or the fear of God. Doubtless many will wear the marks, and thus bear witness of his cruelty, to their graves.

Emaciated countenances, scars, and impediment of speech were the visible marks of the savage and inhuman treatment which they received from the hand of M'Kelpin. Let detestation be written upon his character as legibly as the marks of depravity are to be seen in his visage, and it shall be a lesson to his posterity to flee from iniquity and follow the path of virtue. He excelled in nothing but cruelty and inhumanity, and was superior to none except in the most nefarious acts of iniquity, tyranny, and oppression. His highest ambition appeared to be to "heap up wrath against the day of wrath," and prepare himself to receive "vengeance due to them that know not God, and obey not the gospel of our Lord Jesus Christ, who shall be punished with everlasting destruction." He appeared, involuntarily, to verify the truth of the proverb, "He that is soon angry dealeth foolishly; and a man of wicked devices is hated." Out of the abundance of the heart he publicly declared "that he had taken more comfort in afflicting the prisoners four days than he had four years' time previous." This declaration requires no additional proof to convince every mind susceptible of the least sympathetic affection that he was possessed of no better disposition than the infernal spirits, and must be sufficient to stamp his name with infamy; and, at the same time, excite commiseration in the heart of every person who realizes it is by grace, and not by works, that he is saved from falling into the like wickedness. Nor let any man boast of his good works, knowing it is the gift of God to possess charity.

When we review this awful though faint description of the conduct of M'Kelpin, who enjoyed the advantages of civilization and was favored with the joyful tidings of "peace on earth and good will towards men," filled with anger and revenge, nature cries within us, "Curse the wretch!" But when the meekness and pity of the Savior in his dying agonies upon the shameful and accursed tree are suffered to find a place in our bosoms, we are led to cry, with him, "Father, forgive!" And though the conflict between revenge and forgiving mercy be strong, yet the latter will surely prevail whenever she is properly commanded and led by the Spirit of truth.

I would not intimate that I have the power of necromancy, or pretend to possess a spirit of divination; but, from the authority of holy writ, "this is the portion of a wicked man with God, and the heritage of oppressors, which they shall receive of the Almighty. If his children be multiplied, it is for the sword; and his offspring shall not be satisfied with bread. Those that remain of him shall be buried in death, and his widows shall not weep. Though he heap up silver as the dust, and prepare raiment as the clay, he may prepare it, but the just shall put it on, and the innocent shall divide the silver." I shall therefore leave this great disturber of peace and oppressor of the afflicted to receive from the hand of "Him, who doeth all things well," the punishment due to his wickedness, or share in the mercy offered to the truly penitent, hoping that he may have already, by deep repentance, found forgiveness, or will, before his death, if he is yet living, taste the sweetness of redeeming grace.

He tarried not long on the island, though much longer than he was desired, when another took his office whose name I do not recollect, who manifested a disposition for peace, establishing good order, appeared to have a regard to the laws of justice, humanity, and benevolence, restored tranquillity among the prisoners, and reconciliation between them and the guard.

Could I recollect the name of this person, I would present him to the public as a character worthy of imitation; and as "peacemakers shall be called the children of God," I think I am authorized by the Holy Scriptures to call him by that dignified and honorable title.

In the spring, complaint was made to the British provincial government against the base M'Kelpin, which resulted only in his exclusion from the service of the army with disgrace. The long and successful rebellion of the colonies had greatly exasperated the British; and M'Kelpin, being a strong adherent to their government, loyal to his majesty, and having been harshly treated for his toryism, doubtless the court by which he was tried was strongly though unjustly biased in his favor, which greatly ameliorated his punishment.

In seedtime we were allowed the privilege to sow garden seeds and plant corn. This gave us a prospect of being furnished with not only a more full supply but a greater variety of food, if it should prove our unhappy lot to be kept in confinement another winter. It also gave the prisoners an opportunity to use proper exercise to preserve health and prevent disease—a consideration of no small importance. But, disaffected by our former treatment, and fearing that the afflictions we had once received would again be laid upon us, many chose to hazard their lives by an attempt to swim down the rapids. Some thus succeeded in making their escape, while others only plunged themselves into the jaws of death.

This caused the confinement of all who were left behind. The British now set about encompassing our barracks with pickets or barricades, by setting posts in the ground adjoining each other and fastening them together.

Discovering what they were about to do, several of the prisoners, among whom I was myself, resolved to make our endeavors to effect our escape before they had completed the barricade and encircled our camp, which would deprive us of the liberty of the island. We accordingly collected some logs together on the lower part of the island for a raft, carried some provisions for our sustenance on the way home, secreted it near the logs, and, at an hour when we supposed all were at rest, we started, but had not gone far when we espied one of the soldiers upon the bank of the river employed in dressing some fish. We then returned to our barracks. Our attempt to escape now became known to some of our fellow-prisoners by discovering our absence, who betrayed our object to our keepers, thus courting favor by the deeds of treachery. Having these suspicions, we improved an opportunity to bring back our provisions; and the next day gave proof that our suspicions were well founded, as they then went and rolled all the logs off that part of the island.

We still were determined to use every exertion and watch for an opportunity to effect our escape from confinement while we saw their labors to prevent us. We sought, but sought in vain. Time rolled away, till we found ourselves enclosed with pickets, which rendered it almost impossible to make our escape, as we were not allowed to go without this enclosure unattended by the guard, and that, too, in the daytime only.

We were allowed to go in the daytime, attended by one or two of the guard, and hoe our corn and garden roots. But this afforded us no opportunity for escape, as it was impossible to swim the current on either side of the island undiscovered by the guard or the soldiers stationed in the fort opposite the island. The prisoners, as may well be supposed, had long been very uneasy and discontented; but, as is usually the case, a sense of being confined caused still more disquietude in their minds, and excited an eager desire to be freed from bondage.

The yard which was surrounded by the pickets was about ten or fifteen rods wide and nearly forty rods long, extending lengthwise of the stream. They completed the yard some time in the month of July, 1782. Having encouragement of receiving our discharge, by exchange, often held out to us, and seeing little prospect of succeeding in the hazardous attempt to escape from our confinement, we long waited with great impatience for the approach of that desirable event, and wholly neglected to use any exertion to gain our liberty by flight. But we at length perceived that their object in giving us repeated encouragement of being exchanged was only to dally us with the fond hopes of soon seeing better days, and thus amuse our minds with fancied prospects, while they should be enabled to rivet our chains or privately assassinate some undistinguished number of us. Of this design we had abundant proof, or at least of a disposition to abuse their power by rendering it subservient to the most despicable actions and wicked purposes; for, finding one of the prisoners alone in the evening, a gang of them took him, put a rope round his neck, threatening to stab him to the heart if he made any noise, and were about to hang him, when one of the company, staring him in the face, with a tone of disappointment cried out, "O, this is not the one!" They then took the rope off his neck and let him go.

This manifested to the prisoners either a determination among the guard to waylay some of us, or a wish to trifle with their authority by creating fear in our minds and thus torment the afflicted.

As we were sensible that the guard, if disposed, which we little doubted, might assassinate one or more of the prisoners, and, consigning the body to the waters of the river, keep the transaction hid from the knowledge of any person who should not be engaged in the horrid deed, we were led ever afterwards to take the precaution never to be found alone in the dark unarmed with a large scalping knife, which we kept in our camp, and which served as a dagger and weapon of defence against a violent attack of nocturnal enemies. Having long been flattered with the prospect of soon being set at liberty, and discovering an intention among the guard privately to assassinate some unknown number of us, we resolved to make another attempt to effect our escape, and thus free ourselves from their brutal tyranny and unhallowed pretences.

We had once paid several dollars to one of the guard to suffer us to pass through the gate, should he find an opportunity; but never had the good fortune even to see him again.

The plan we adopted was in itself extremely precarious as to its success, and afforded so little encouragement, even to those who seemed to be most anxious to obtain their freedom, that few would engage in the enterprise, believing it would be a fruitless attempt to obtain our object, which would only cost us pain and bring upon us more sore trials and far greater afflictions.

Had we been confined upon the main land, where liberty from the prison would have afforded us a chance to retreat from danger, though we should be obliged even to pass the gates of a city surrounded with enemies, having our hands bound in irons and our feet fettered with chains, yet our prospects of success in our attempt to escape had still been brighter than now presented to our view; for then our deliverance from prison might have given us a passport to the wilderness free from danger; but now our freedom from those walls of wretchedness incurred the penalty of death, which was annexed to our escape if overtaken, and brought us to "troubled waters," which seemed to promise death inevitable to all who should attempt to pass the current even with well-fitted boats; while we had nothing in our power but logs, fastened together with ropes.

Our plan was, to dig a passage under ground that should extend beyond the pickets, which stood about twenty feet from the barracks. It had been our practice during the summer to hang up blankets around the bunks in which we slept, to prevent the flies from troubling us while we reposed upon our couch in the daytime.

We now again hung up the blankets around one of our bunks in a corner of the room, though not to prevent being disturbed by flies, but to hide ourselves from the face of "serpents that will bite without enchantment; and a babbler, which is no better."

Fearing the consequence of making our object known to the prisoners generally, we determined to keep it a profound secret to all except the number who belonged to our room, consisting of twelve. Accordingly, we took up the floor, both of the bunk and barrack, and commenced digging. If any of our fellow-prisoners or the guard happened to come in while one was at work, others would drown the noise of his digging by making some noise with a stick or with their feet, which was easily done without being suspected of the design.

We dug in a perpendicular direction deep enough to have a horizontal course leave the earth between the barracks and the pickets, of sufficient depth to render it safe for the guard to travel over the hole without breaking through. As they had dug a ditch along the back side of the barracks between them and the pickets in order to bank up the walls of the barracks, it became necessary for us to dig a perpendicular course of considerable depth before we could dig horizontally, to prevent any person who might chance to travel in the ditch from breaking in and discovering our plan.

We had no other tool to dig with except a large jackknife; nor, indeed, could we use any other instrument with any advantage when we came to dig in a horizontal line. And, like the animal that makes his abode in the bosom of the earth by digging a subterraneous passage to his gloomy cell, after we had dug a quantity of earth loose, so that we had no room to dig more, we returned backwards, drawing or scraping the dirt we had dug with our hands and arms, which we put under the floor of the barracks.

Our progress, as must readily be perceived, was very slow; though some one of us kept constantly digging except in the hours of sleep and time of taking refreshment, alternately following each other in our turns; having a dress prepared for the purpose which each one wore while at work in this dreary cavern, where we were groping in darkness at noonday. Here we had an opportunity to reflect upon our wretched condition, while our labor itself witnessed our sufferings and discontentment. Here we could perceive the comparative state of him who spiritually "walketh in darkness and hath no light." Here it might, indeed, with propriety be said that silence wept. We succeeded, however, in the prosecution of our design extremely well, finding no obstacle in our way till we had dug under the ditch before mentioned, when a heavy rain fell and filled the ditch full of water, which soaked through the ground into our subterraneous way and filled the hole we had dug completely full. This was truly a great misfortune, which dampened the feelings of every one who had been engaged in the arduous undertaking.

As we had dug considerable distance and advanced nearly to the pickets, had toiled with diligence and expended much labor, we were unwilling to relinquish the task and submit to the idea of continuing in bondage another winter. And we were the more anxious to pursue the undertaking and effect our escape, because the infamous M'Daniel, of whom I have spoken, had now returned and resumed his command over us, which gave us greater reason to fear that we should again be compelled to undergo those tortures which he had once inflicted.

But it now became impossible any longer to keep the matter secret as we had done. We therefore made known our object to all the prisoners who were stationed in our line of barracks; and, receiving their universal and respective promises not to divulge the secret to any of the prisoners who were stationed in the other line of barracks,—although few would assist us, considering it labor in vain,—we resolved to persevere in the plan, and, if possible, effect our escape.

We now commenced dipping out the water into a barrel, which we emptied into a ditch that was made to convey our wash water from the barracks into the river. We dipped six barrels' full and emptied it into the ditch, besides a considerable quantity which we put into a clay pit under the barracks where they dug clay for their chimneys; and still there was much left in our way.

The guard, no doubt, supposed we were washing, or they would have suspected us. Nor yet can I account for their stupidity while they saw we were in possession of such a quantity of water, which we brought out of, without carrying into, our barracks.

We were now obliged to lie half buried in mud and water while digging, which chilled our bodies, benumbed our senses, and depressed our spirits.

To prevent being discovered, when we returned from our toil we were under the necessity of washing ourselves in a large tub of water, which we had also placed behind our blankets that were hung up around our bunk; as we now were forced, on account of the mud, to enter upon our subterraneous labor entirely naked. Vain would be the attempt to give a description of my feelings while at work in this dreary cavern, twenty feet under ground, wholly without clothing, half buried in mud, and struggling for liberty.

I was removed from all my friends and relatives the distance of more than three hundred miles, and placed upon an island in the river, on both sides of which the water moved over the ragged rocks with such velocity as to appear white to the eye like a foaming billow, not less than three miles in length. Here I was confined within the power, and exposed to the envy, malice, and resentment, of an implacable enemy. Shrouded in darkness, in the heart of the earth where light was unapproachable, my body lay in the mire, and my mind was overwhelmed with sorrow. If we refrained from digging, we seemed to be threatened with death on every side; and if we continued to dig, our prospect appeared as melancholy as the grave. Fear and trouble were before us; while our absence from the barracks exposed us to the danger of having our plan discovered, which would be sure to bring upon us the most awful tortures, and perhaps even death itself. We chose, however, rather to hazard our lives in an attempt to escape, though doubtful of success, than to risk the consequences of remaining in confinement.

When we arrived to the picket we found it was placed upon a large stone. We then dug to the right, where we found another, which formed an angle with the first. Then, turning to the left, we also found a third. All which seemed to discourage my fellow-laborers, and led them entirely to give up the object. But, being in perfect health and in good spirits myself, I went in with a determination to remove one of these obstacles, if possible, before I returned. We had, by this time, made quite a large cavern near the pickets, which gave me considerable chance to work. After laboring in this cold, dismal place during the space of two hours, I succeeded in removing one of the stones out of the way, and, to my great joy, found that the picket was hollow up a few inches above the ground, which emitted light into this before gloomy but now delightful place. I could verily say with Solomon, "Truly the light is sweet; and a pleasant thing it is to behold the sun."

I then returned and informed my fellow-prisoners of my success, which occasioned transports of joy, raised the desponding, encouraged the faithless, confirmed the doubting, and put new vigor in every breast.

The work was now prosecuted in earnest and soon completed. Animated at the prospect of gaining our liberty, the one who dug last undesignedly broke through the ground and rendered the hole visible to any person who should happen to pass on the outside of the pickets. It now became necessary to devise a plan to secrete the hole from the observation of the guard. To effect this, Mr. Belknap, one of our fellow-prisoners, went to the guard, and, in a dissembling tone, represented to M'Daniel the little prospect we had of being exchanged; that we had long been flattered, and as long waited with anxious expectation, for the approach of such a happy event, but, finding ourselves disappointed, were forced to abandon all hopes of deliverance by exchange that fall; that, under these considerations, the prisoners were resolved to be contented during their confinement on the island till they should find themselves actually set at liberty, when all their hopes would be swallowed up in the full fruition of the object we had so long sought. Consequently we desired the indulgence of an opportunity to secure all our garden seeds, some of which, such as lettuce and mustard, were then ripe and fit to harvest, that we might be enabled to supply ourselves with the like articles the ensuing year, should it be our unhappy case to remain on the island another season.

Pleased with the idea that the prisoners were resolved to be submissive to his requirements, he readily ordered one of the guard to go and attend us while we gathered our lettuce and mustard, whose duty it was to see that no one absconded. Having cut and tied up in small bundles these vegetables, we proceeded to hang them up so as to fill the space between the pickets, and also place them over the hole we had dug, to hide our escape from the sight of the sentinel, who walked over the hole between the pickets and the barracks in which we were stationed. This we accomplished while our unsuspecting attendant was lounging about at a distance from us.

Here we beheld an example of selfishness, discontentment, fear, and deception, actually assuming the appearance of honesty, contentment, and submission.

Knowing that we must separate ourselves into small companies and take different rafts, in order to render our passage down the rapids more safe, we now made choice of our associates to pass the dangerous scene before us. I associated myself with William Clark, of Virginia, John Sprague, of Ballston, New York, and Simeon Belknap, of Randolph, Vermont. We had prepared some food for our sustenance on the way by taking a quantity of flour and mixing it with melted butter, which we put into a small bag made for the purpose. We also had a little salt pork and bread, together with some parched corn and black pepper.

Those of us who had been engaged in digging had previously furnished ourselves with ropes, by cutting our blankets into strings and twisting them together; while those who had believed our attempt to be vain and foolish had neither provided themselves with provisions, ropes, or materials for a raft, and were, therefore, unable to improve the opportunity which now presented to effect their escape.

But they could not forbear collecting in small companies and whispering together to devise plans for escape, which raised suspicions in the minds of the guard that the prisoners were entering into some plot either to make their escape or to raise a mutiny in the camp. Under these apprehensions, which took rise from no other source but from the conduct of those who had been made privy to our undertaking, and would neither assist us in the work nor prepare themselves to make their escape, M'Daniel ordered that, "if any prisoner should be found attempting to make his escape or be guilty of any misconduct that night, he should not be spared alive."

We commenced digging on the 24th of August, 1782; and having dug a passage under ground the distance of twenty-two feet and a half with no other tool but a jackknife, on the night of the 10th of September following, after waiting till nine o'clock, when the roll was called and all was still, we tied our ropes to our packs and crawled out, drawing our packs after us. I was preceded by six of my fellow-prisoners, who, after crawling through the hole, which was nearly half filled with mud, made a path in the grass, as they crawled down the banks of the river, which resembled that of a log having been drawn through the mud.

The moon shone bright. The sentinel was walking directly across the hole just as I was about to crawl out, when he cried out, "All's well!" Thought I, "Be it so; continue the cry, if you please." My head at this time was not more than a yard from his feet. I crawled on, and was followed by about twenty more, who were our fellow-laborers.

As we had been allowed to go out of our enclosure in the daytime to hoe our corn and garden roots and get our wood, attended by one of the guard, we had improved the opportunity, and selected some logs for a raft to which we could go without difficulty. Clark, Belknap, Sprague, and myself now separated ourselves from the rest of the prisoners and remained together, sharing equally in all the sufferings through which we were called to pass.

We took a large scalping knife with us and a pocket compass, together with a tinder box and fireworks. We rolled a large log into the river on the upper part of the north side of the island, on each side of which we placed another; then, putting sticks across both ends of them, underneath and on the upper side, opposite each other, we tied all of them together with our blanket ropes, and fastening our packs thereon, which contained our provision, &c., we then sat one on each corner and set sail down the rapids.

Death in its most frightful form now seemed to threaten us, and the foaming billows pointed us to a watery grave. Guided only by the current, sometimes floating over rocks, sometimes buried in the water, with little hope of again being carried out alive, we passed down the raging stream with the greatest rapidity imaginable, clinging to our logs respectively, sensible that, under the guidance of divine Providence, our only ground of hope rested in our adhesion to the raft.

We passed down the river about nine miles, when we were enabled to reach shore. We landed on the north side of the river about two hours before day, with not a dry thread in our clothes, chilled with the cold and trembling with fear. Our bread had all washed to a jelly and been rendered wholly unfit to eat. None of our provision remained fit to carry with us except a little parched corn, which was in a small, wooden bottle, some salt pork, and our buttered flour, which we found to be waterproof. Our compass was also rendered useless; which was indeed a great misfortune to us, as the want of it protracted our journey through the woods many days. We marched up the river till daybreak, when we discovered that we were near the fort opposite the island. We then turned north into the woods, which led us into a swamp, where we encamped under some old tree tops that had fallen together, about one mile from the fort, which formed no shelter from rain, but merely hid us from our expected pursuers. We plainly heard the report of the alarm guns on the morning of the 11th of September, which announced to us the discovery of what had cost us great pains, and evinced, to all who should behold the place, our love of liberty and resolution to obtain it.

We remained under these tree tops three days and two nights without going ten rods from the place, having nothing to eat but salt pork, parched corn, and our buttered flour, together with a few kernels of black pepper; for the want of which last I think we must have perished, as it rained with a mixture of snow every day and night sufficiently to keep us completely wet all the time.

Having been so harshly treated by the British, and knowing that "confidence in an unfaithful man in time of trouble is like a broken tooth and a foot out of joint," we resolved to make ourselves known to no one; and like the Ishmaelites of old, while we had reason to suppose that every man's hand was against us, we were determined to put our own hands against every man who should come in our way.

Destitute of food sufficient to supply us through the long woods we were to pass to reach our homes, we were determined to replenish our stores before we crossed the River St. Lawrence, as there were but few settlements on the south side of the river in that part of the country. We were, therefore, under the necessity of staying about there till they had done searching for us.

On the night of the third day after our escape we ventured to take up our march, and travelled till we came to a stream which we supposed emptied into the River St. Lawrence at the fort; but we afterwards found it to be only a branch of that stream. I waded into it, and found it was so deep that we could not ford it. I therefore returned, and we encamped for the night. Our sufferings this night were almost insupportable; as it was a cold, frosty night, and we were wholly exposed, having nothing about us except what was completely wet, without a shelter, and destitute of fire.

On the morning of the 14th, benumbed and chilled with the cold, we found a place where we forded the stream, and travelled till we came to another; and by mistaking the former, we supposed this to empty itself into the river above the fort. We followed the current of this stream till about dark, when we came in sight of a settlement. After waiting till about nine o'clock at night we ventured to approach a little nearer, when to our utter astonishment we heard the drum beat, which gave us assurance that we were near the fort. Finding ourselves so near, we concluded to cross the stream at the nearest fording-place. In passing off we went through the commanding officer's garden; and I pulled up a hill of his potatoes and carried them along with me.

We then went into the road and followed up the River St. Lawrence about four miles. We had not proceeded far, however, before we came to a boat lying at anchor in the river, near the shore. I waded in towards it till I heard men in it snoring in their sleep, when I quickly made my retreat. We then went on till we came to the house of a Frenchman, as we supposed by his speech, who, just as we came up, opened the door and hailed us. Turning into his lot, we went to his barn and endeavored to find some creature to kill. We found one cow. As we were approaching towards her, two large dogs came at us with great rage, and, barking most furiously, appeared to be determined to bite us. The old Frenchman again came to the door and hailed us. Fearing that soldiers might be quartered there, we retreated as fast as we could, keeping an eye upon the dogs, and swinging our staves at them to keep them from biting us, while the old Frenchman was trying to set them on. The ground was descending as we retreated; and while we were all moving together very fast, having our eyes partially turned upon the dogs, we ran against a fence, slightly laid up, and threw down many lengths, which made such a rattling that it terrified the dogs and immediately put them upon their retreat, as much affrighted as they had been outrageous.

Trembling for our safety, we kept in the fields back of the street; while the dogs continued their barking as if determined to arouse our enemies from their slumbers and cause us to be taken. They succeeded, at least, in exciting all the dogs in the neighborhood to engage in the general alarm, and seemed anxious to maintain a constant echo in the surrounding atmosphere. They were busily employed at every house, and sometimes in great earnest, as we passed along the distance of several miles.

At length we came to a number of cattle in a field not far from the road, among which we found a two-year-old heifer, very tame and in good flesh.

We had long been lurking about, waiting for the agitation of the public mind to abate, that we might have opportunity to obtain some provision before we entered into the wide wilderness through which we were expecting to pass; and as the favored moment had now arrived, we agreed that Belknap should go in search of a boat to convey us over the Lake St. Francis, near which we found the cattle; that Sprague should stand with our scalping knife to defend against every foe; while Clark and myself should kill the heifer and procure a quantity of meat. By the help of a little salt I soon succeeded in catching the heifer; and, taking her by the horns and nose, I instantly flung her down, when Clark cut her throat with a large jackknife; and, not waiting for her to die or even spending time to skin her, we took off a gammon and left her bleeding. Belknap had now returned and informed us that he had found a boat, to which we immediately resorted, carrying with us our unskinned beef, the booty we had desired for many days, leaving the owner of the heifer to seek his recompense where he could find it; willing, however, he should share with us in his beef by taking what we left.

We were not insensible that, if he were a British subject, we had abundantly compensated his loss to his government by our own starvation; or, if he were a friend to the unfortunate, he could not lament his loss, since he had thus far contributed to feed the hungry without even knowing what his right hand did. Nor, indeed, did we trouble ourselves, while we ruminated upon the affair, concerning what might be the cogitations of the owner; since we had obtained the meat, and thus answered our own purpose.

Having entered the boat with all our baggage, the moon shining bright, we set out upon the lake, steering for the south shore. We had advanced but little distance when a breeze arose from the north-west and drifted us ahead with great violence, every wave dashing the water into our boat.

It now became necessary that two of us should dip the water from our boat with our hats as fast as possible, while the other two rowed for the shore with the greatest exertion. The wind increased. The boat was fast filling in spite of all we could do. Every wave, to human view, brought us by rapid strides to the arms of death and presented to us a watery grave. But, through the wonderful goodness of the great Preserver of men, we succeeded in landing just as our boat had filled with water. Having fastened it to the shore we went into the woods, struck up a fire, skinned our beef and cut it into thin slices, which we partially roasted on sticks by the fire, and then lay down to sleep. This was the first time we had been to any fire since we left Prison Island. We had lain secreted in bushes and old tree tops; wandered in the darkness of the night, exposed to the inclemency of the weather; forded streams of water up to our necks, constantly and completely wet; hungry, and chilled with cold; filled with fear and anxiety for our safety during the space of four days and five nights, including the night in which we made our escape.

Destruction and misery often appeared in our way. Death frequently stared us in the face, threatening to make us his prey, but seemed to be held from falling upon us by the finger of God.

On the morning of the 15th of September, (the fifth day after we escaped,) supposing we had landed upon an island, we began to seek how we should get off without being discovered by the inhabitants on the northern shores of the lake or by those who might happen to be upon the waters. Happily we found, by travelling into the woods, that we were upon a peninsula, joined to the main land by an isthmus not more than eight or ten feet wide. This was a circumstance greatly in our favor, as we should otherwise have been under the necessity of exposing ourselves to the view of our enemies, or waiting for the night to cover our escape.

We now set out, directing our course nearly south-east, for the American fort at Pittsford, a town situated on Otter Creek, in the western part of the State of Vermont.

Our companion, Mr. Clark, had been much accustomed to travelling in the woods, having been engaged in the business of surveying in the western part of the United States at the time he was taken by the Indians. We therefore chose him to be our leader through the wilderness and our pilot to a more favored country.

We travelled all the first day over low, marshy land, timbered with cedar, but were unable to find any water to drink either in running brooks or by digging; for the want of which we suffered much, being thirsty as well as hungry, and greatly fatigued. Wishing to escape the vigilance of our expected pursuers, we travelled with great speed, which, together with our living on flesh alone, doubtless occasioned a far greater degree of thirst than we should have felt had we been supplied with bread. The next day we found water in great plenty. We crossed many streams of considerable size; some by fording, although of such depth as to reach to our shoulders: others we crossed by making a small raft sufficient to bear one of us with our baggage; while the other three stripped, and, hanging by one hand to the raft, swam by her side.

After wandering in the wilderness during the space of ten days,—sometimes progressing on our journey, sometimes lounging in suspense, doubting which course to take, and waiting for the clouds to be dispelled, that the sun might appear to enlighten our path and guide our way,—we arrived at Lake Champlain with our clothes nearly torn from our bodies, emaciated with hunger and fatigued with the daily toil and long deprivation of the comforts of civilized life. During these ten days we saw no other human being, nor heard his voice, beheld his footsteps, or the works of his hand. We lived almost wholly on flesh, like the carnivorous race, and, like them, reposed upon the ground, equally fearing the face of man, suspicious of his design, and dreading his approach as we did the instrument of death.

While we one day lay encamped by the fire, waiting for the appearance of the sun, we were aroused from our sleep by the supposed report of a musket. Ignorant of the source whence it came, and fearing to make immediate flight lest we should flee into the hands of our enemies, we prepared ourselves to march, and were endeavoring to espy the foe, when a similar noise, proceeding from the bursting of a stone heated by the fire, relieved our minds from fear, and filled our bosoms with joy at the happy disappointment of expected danger.

Soon after we arrived at Lake Champlain we found a part of an old flat-bottomed boat, which we fitted up, for the purpose of conveying us across the lake, by lashing a log on each side with bark and withs.

At about sunset we went aboard and set sail to cross the lake. We had proceeded nearly half way across, when the wind arose against us and baffled all our exertions to proceed farther. After laboring till about midnight without success, and fearing we should be taken by the British if we remained on the water till light, we concluded to row back to the shore we left and relinquish the idea of crossing the lake that night. We had continued upon the water till a tempest arose, and the wind blew from various directions, shifting its course every few minutes; and our strength had become almost exhausted, being faint for want of food, insomuch that we could hardly move. We labored with diligence and with all our might till daybreak, having nothing to use for oars except such sticks as we found in the woods and prepared for the purpose with a jackknife. We were now enabled to reach the same shore from which we started, though several miles farther north. Our clothes were completely wet, and our strength so far gone that neither of us could scarcely go.

In this wretched state, stupefied and chilled with the cold, so faint and tired that we could hardly move, we crept a few rods into the woods, built a fire, and laid down upon the ground.

I never suffered so much fatigue, in the same space of time in my life, as I did this night; nor would I have believed I could endure as much, with so little strength, without perishing. Language is too feeble to express, nor can imagination conceive, the sufferings we underwent.

We had but little provision left, and were compelled to curtail our former allowance, so that we should be enabled to subsist and continue our journey till we could reach the desired country.

Having rested from the wearisome and fruitless labors of the night till nearly sunset the next day, we resolved to travel on the west side of the lake till we should come to a narrow place where we could well hope for success in an attempt to cross. We resumed our march and travelled a few miles that night, then camped down and waited for the morning.

The next day we came to the River Saranac, which empties into Lake Champlain at a place now called Plattsburg, in the State of New York. We heard the noise of the British engaged in chopping a few rods up the river, while we crossed it between them and the lake, not far from its mouth.

After we crossed the river we travelled a small distance and encamped for the night in a valley which was in the form of a basin. We followed up the lake upon the western shore; crossed Duck Creek, River-au-Sable, Salmon River, and Gilliland's Creek; when we came to a place called Split Rock, where the lake is narrow, which afforded us a prospect of succeeding if we attempted to cross. We then went to work to build a raft, and while engaged, a little before sunset, espied a British armed vessel making towards us from the south. We went into the bushes and lay secreted from their view, though they were so visible to us that we could see their red coats, and even count the buttons upon them, while they sailed around at a small distance from us, apparently for amusement, and then returned again to the south, out of our sight, without discovering us.

We then went to work, completed our raft at dark, set sail across the lake, and safely landed in a few hours at a place now called Charlotte, in the State of Vermont. We were, however, ignorant at that time both of the name of the place and of its local situation. Being yet in a strange wilderness, we knew not which way to direct our course to reach inhabitants. Indeed, all that prompted us to go forward was the information we had received that there were settlements near some part of this lake. But we were wholly ignorant what way to take that should enable us to find them. Supposing ourselves to be between the mouth of Onion River and Otter Creek, we concluded to steer in a south-east direction, which we supposed would bring us to Pittsford Fort. We travelled into the woods a few rods and lay down for the night. In the morning we resumed our march, and had not gone far before we came to an old log house, which had long been abandoned, and, by the long continuance of the war, had become greatly decayed.

We however found a few beans, which had probably been there a number of years, and were covered with mould. As our provision was mostly gone and we were extremely hungry, we took and parched them, as we would corn, by the fire, which gave some relish to the twigs, roots, and berries that had already, for some days, composed our principal food.

Our clothes were almost torn from our mangled bodies by the bushes, logs, and trees; and the blood that gushed from our naked and wornout feet witnessed, in every track we made, the pains we suffered.

Parts of our stockings still remained about our feet; and, having a needle (but no thread) with us, we ravelled off the tops of them and sewed our tattered rags together as much as possible, to defend our bodies from the inclemency of the weather.

Our daily allowance of the food we brought with us from Prison Island was now reduced to about an inch square of salt pork and as much of our buttered flour as we could twice put upon the point of a large jackknife. We had eaten all our beef and parched corn.

We dug roots of various kinds and ate them, together with birch and other twigs. Spikenard roots, which we roasted by the fire, comprised the greatest part of our subsistence. We found several small frogs, which we killed and ate with great delight. But we could find only a few of them, though we searched diligently. Their meat tasted exceedingly sweet and delicious. We also found means to catch several small fish from a little rivulet which we crossed; but could not obtain more than two or three, although we spent much time and used every exertion in our power.

Some time after we had dressed our fish and had advanced considerable distance, we espied a bear upon a tree a few rods ahead of us. We hastened to the foot of the tree, in view of killing her, as she descended, by stabbing her with our large scalping knife. But, on examination, we found the knife was left at the place of dressing the fish, which frustrated our plan and blighted our hopes of obtaining any meat.

Disappointment was now added to hunger and distress, and our faint and wearied bodies were hardly able to support the dreadful weight of sorrow which hung over our minds.

We however continued to keep a south-east course till we reached the top of the mountains lying between Onion River and Otter Creek, when, looking back, we could see the lake in fair view. Being so faint for want of food that we could hardly step, and seeing no prospect of obtaining any, it seemed as if death must be our inevitable fate. We had travelled seven or eight days, and had subsisted the whole time mostly upon the spontaneous productions of the country. The season for berries was nearly gone, though we were able to find some.

Our natures seemed to waste away and leave nothing but death to stare us in the face. Winter was fast approaching, while we were almost naked, destitute, and forlorn. O the wretched condition of those whose lot it is to be cast into the wilderness and left to wander upon the dark mountains of despair! I could feelingly adopt the language of Job, and say, "Terrors are turned upon me: they pursue my soul as the wind; and my welfare passeth away as a cloud. When I looked for good, then evil came unto me; and when I waited for light, there came darkness. I am a brother to dragons and a companion to owls; for I have eaten ashes like bread and mingled my drink with weeping."

Had we seen any prospect of soon finding the house of a friend, or of obtaining provision in any other way before we should arrive among inhabitants, we could not have denied ourselves at once to eat the little provision we had in our packs while we suffered so much by hunger on our way.

The barren mountains and rocky cliffs of Bristol, Ripton, and Hancock, the dismal plain of Chataugua, and the waters of Champlain witnessed the cries of our sufferings; while our steps traced in blood the distress we endured.

We wandered from mountain to mountain and from valley to valley, keeping at a distance from the lake, lest we should fall into the hands of the British, who had command of the lake at that time. Sorrow, hunger, and bitterness of soul were our constant attendants through the day; and the approach of the night only increased our miseries and multiplied our sighs and groanings.

Though we slept, it was for trouble; and if we continued to roam the wilderness we found no comfort, and our strength failed. If we slumbered, it was upon the brink of the grave, and it would not feed us. While our hunger increased, our hopes of relief grew dim.

Seeing no prospect of ever finding the habitations of friends, our companions, Clark and Sprague, like the lepers of old, "said to one another, Why sit we here until we die?" If we say we will pursue our journey, "we shall die; and if we sit still here, we die also." They therefore resolved to return to the lake if they could get there, and deliver themselves up into the hands of the British.

They were both possessed of true courage, and a noble, generous spirit. But they were wholly ignorant of the country east of Lake Champlain, and consequently had less to encourage them than Belknap and myself. They were "unwilling," said they, "that we should either return or remain with them, if we could ever reach inhabitants. But to go forward was apparent death, even if inhabitants might be found by two or three days' travel; as we are so weak we can hardly go, and still growing weaker." They requested us to leave them to be food for wild beasts or a prey to an exasperated foe. But the tender feelings of human sensibility forbade us to leave them; and Belknap and myself persuaded them to persevere and remain with us to the end by dealing out to them an extra allowance of provision, on condition that I should take the lead and be their pilot; to which I consented.

It being nearly night, we encamped till morning, when we concluded to change our course and steer nearly a south-south-westerly direction. We travelled on moderately, fearful of the event, till about noon, when, being some rods forward of my companions, I was so fortunate as to come to a road. Of this I notified my languishing companions, famishing with hunger and groaning under the weight of their wretchedness, which occasioned transports of joy, gladdened their hearts, and invigorated their bodies; yea, it "shed happiness around us and banished misery before us." For we could say with David, that we had "wandered in the wilderness, in a solitary way, and found no city to dwell in. Hungry and thirsty, our souls fainted within us. Then we cried unto the Lord in our trouble, and he delivered us out of our distresses; and he led us forth by the right way, that we might go to a city of habitation."

Animated with the prospect of soon finding inhabitants, we travelled on the road with joy and delight. Our hopes of again seeing our friends became brightened, and our expectations greatly strengthened our weak and trembling limbs. We soon came in sight of an old horse, and an old mare with a sucking colt by her side. As they were in a valley some distance from the road, we concluded not to go after them, hoping soon to find inhabitants, where we should be enabled also to find friends, who would lend the hand of charity. We therefore travelled on, and soon came to a stream, but could not determine whether it was Otter Creek or only a branch of it. If it were a branch, we knew we ought to follow the current till we came to the creek. But to follow the current of the creek itself would lead us directly to the lake, where we should be exposed to the British.

We however thought it most prudent to follow down the stream, and soon came to its mouth, and still were left in doubt whether the stream into which the first we discovered emptied itself was Otter Creek or some other branch.

As it began to draw near sunset, and seeing no prospect of finding inhabitants that night, we resolved to return to the place where we came to the first stream, having there found the walls of an old log house. Clark and myself went and procured the horses and colt; while Belknap and Sprague struck up a fire and built a camp.

Having returned with the horses and confined them in the old log house, we killed and dressed the colt and roasted some of the meat upon sticks by the fire and ate it; and surely "it was pleasant to the taste." Indeed, I never ate any meat of so delicious a flavor, although without bread, salt, or sauce of any kind.

The next morning we started with our old horse and coltless mare, and travelled till after the middle of the day, when we came to the place we passed about noon the day preceding. We were confident it was the same place, by finding some spikenard roots which we had thrown away soon after we found the road.

Being lost, and knowing not whether to turn to the right hand or to the left, having obtained a new supply of meat, by which we had been much refreshed, and as the sun had been invisible to us for several days, we concluded to tarry there through the day and encamp for the night, hoping the sun would rise clear the next morning, which would enable us the better to determine what course to take.

While we were patrolling about the fields, which appeared to have been unoccupied and but partially cultivated during the long war, we found a large yard of turnips.

We then prepared our camp, built a fire, and, having procured some turnips, kept continually roasting them successively during the night, first sleeping a little and then eating; thus alternately refreshing ourselves by sleep and eating cold meat with roasted turnips till the approach of day. As we had long lived upon the spontaneous growth of the wilderness, and had not only been almost entirely destitute of bread and meat, but wholly deprived of every cultivated vegetable, we were conscious that it would be injurious, and even dangerous, to eat immediately all we might crave for the night.

We therefore chose to satiate our hunger in a measure by piecemeals, while we truly feasted upon that kind of fare which was undoubtedly, of all kinds of food, the best adapted to our wretched condition and craving appetites. In the morning the sky was clear, and the sun rose, to every one of us, directly in the *west*. We now discovered the cause of becoming lost; and, feeling much refreshed and strengthened, we took our horses and directed our course according to the sun, diametrically against our own ideas of the true point of compass. We had not proceeded far when we came to three other horses, which we took, leaving the old mare for the benefit of the owner.

After travelling till about noon we came to a man chopping in the woods. Seeing us all on horseback, with bark bridles and no saddles, having on coats made of Indian blankets, which were all in rags, with beards an inch long, and each one of us armed with a cudgel, the trembling woodcutter stood in dreadful awe, with his axe raised above his shoulder, dreading our approach, but fearing to try his success in an attempt to escape; while we drew near, rejoicing that we had once more arrived where we could behold the face of one whose hand should not be against us, and against whom we were not compelled for our safety to put our own hands.

We were not much surprised, though very sorry, to find our friend so grievously alarmed while we only desired his friendship. We informed him of our wretched condition, and besought him to be our friend, with tears of joy and tenderness trickling down our emaciated cheeks. Finding we were not his enemies, but the subjects of his pity and tender compassion, bursting into tears of sympathy at the short relation we gave him of our sufferings, he invited us to go with him and he would lead us to Pittsford Fort, which was only about one mile distant, where we should be made welcome to every thing necessary for our comfort.

We soon arrived at the fort. It was now about one o'clock in the afternoon. We were received with the greatest marks of sympathy and commiseration and treated with every respect due to our wretchedness and want. And though justice demands that I should acknowledge the generous display of philanthropic zeal, as well as selfish curiosity, common on such occasions, yet I could not forbear to notice with pain that cold indifference for the miseries of others, commonly observable in those who have long been familiar with scenes of wretchedness and woe, which was manifested by some, and especially by the commander of the fort, on our arrival at that place.

Not long after we arrived at the fort the owners of the horses came up, carrying their saddles upon their backs. They had been out for the purpose of surveying land, and had turned out their horses to feed. After hearing a short account of our sufferings and being made acquainted with our deplorable condition, they readily replied, with seeming compassion, that they were only sorry we had not been so fortunate as to find their saddles likewise.

After wandering in the wilderness twenty-two days, we arrived at the fort on the 2d day of October, 1782, having forded rivers of water up to our shoulders; traversing through dismal swamps, the habitations of beasts of prey; and climbing mountains of rocks, where no human eye could pity or friends console us; making the earth our bed of repose for the night, and extreme anxiety our constant companion through the day; nearly starved, and almost naked; little expecting ever again to see the faces of our friends or to behold those habitations which witnessed our juvenile years, where we enjoyed the kind embraces of tender and affectionate mothers and the paternal care of indulgent fathers; expecting every day to see the approach of that hour when our spirits should be called to leave our bodies in a howling wilderness to become food for wild beasts, and our friends to lament our absence, ignorant of our end. After enduring all this, yea, more than pen can describe or language express, who can tell our joy and gratitude when we came to behold a "city of habitation" and the abodes of plenty? What heart would not palpitate for exceeding great joy at such an event? Who could forbear to speak forth praise to the great Preserver of men on such an occasion?

Would not every heart, susceptible of the least impression, acknowledge the hand of the Almighty in so great a deliverance?

Instead of making our bed upon the cold ground, with our clothes wet and our bodies benumbed, we could now enjoy sweet repose by the fireside, sheltered from storms and surrounded with friends. Instead of feeding upon frogs and the spontaneous growth of uncultivated nature, subsisting on roots, twigs, and bark, we could now taste the fruits of labor and industry, and feast upon the bounties of Heaven. Instead of wandering through a lonely wilderness, with our cheeks wet with tears of sorrow, almost overwhelmed with despair, we could now travel through a country of civilization free from enemies, and receive support from the hand of charity.

After sharing in the benevolence of many individuals, and receiving every token of friendship from the garrison at the fort, as they were expecting soon to be attacked by the British, we were advised to travel on still farther that night, that we might be the more safe from the grasp of the enemy.

We therefore proceeded on towards Rutland several miles, when we obtained lodgings in the house of a "poor widow," who furnished us with the best food her house afforded, of which we ate heartily. Having long been without bread of any kind, and being now furnished with a full supply of good wheat bread, it seemed as if we should die with the effect of eating it. It lay like lead in our stomachs, and caused us the most agonizing distress for some hours, while we rolled upon the floor with bitter groanings, although we had denied ourselves the satisfaction of eating the half of what our appetites craved. But our extreme hunger prevented the exercise of prudence and economy in the choice of that kind of food which was best adapted to our wretched condition. Nor did we wait long to consult about the propriety or impropriety of eating any thing we found within our reach. Our avidity for food, however, soon abated, when we found no injury to result from eating all we desired.

We made our escape on the night of the 10th of September, arrived at Lake Champlain in about ten days, and came to the fort on the night of the 2d of October following; having been in the wilderness twenty-two days, without speaking to any other person except our own company. It is true, we had seen some of our species at a distance from us, though with terror and dismay, fearing their approach as we should have done that of a voracious animal ready to devour us.

In a few days we arrived at Bennington, in Bennington county, Vermont, where we were employed till we had acquired, by our own labor and the benevolence of others, some money sufficient to enable us to prosecute our journey to Connecticut.

Having travelled many days through the woods almost destitute of any covering for our feet, they had become very sore, which prevented our going far in a day.

Assisted by the hand of charity and by means of occasional labor on the way, we were enabled to reach our friends. Being destined to different places, our companions, Clark and Sprague, separated from us at Bennington. By a mutual participation of sufferings, we had acquired that affection for each other which will remain, I trust, till death. Having suffered many hardships and endured many trials together, having been rescued from many dangers and delivered out of many troubles, sharing equally in hunger, pains, and distress, as well as in the joys resulting from our deliverance, we now reluctantly parted, affectionately taking our leave, perhaps never again to see each other till we shall meet in that world where "the weary be at rest. There the prisoners rest together; they hear not the voice of the oppressor. The small and great are there; and the servant is free from his master."

And may it not be the unspeakable infelicity of either of us to fail of "entering into that rest because of unbelief."

Belknap and I continued our course together to Ellington, in Connecticut, where our friends resided. We arrived there on the 17th of October, 1782, being just two years from the day I was taken by the Indians at Randolph. What pen can describe the mutual joy which was felt by parents and children on our arrival? Truly our fathers, "seeing us while yet a great way off, ran and fell upon our necks and kissed us." Behold now the affection of a father. See him shed the tear of compassion. Hear him say, "This my son was dead, and is alive again; he was lost, and is found." See him "begin to be merry;" nor think it strange that the fatted calf should be killed.

Behold a kind father in tears of joy, and a tender step-mother kindly embracing the subject of her husband's former grief, but present delight. See "the best robe" cast around him, with "the ring upon his hand and the shoes upon his feet." See brothers and sisters surrounding the returned brother. Hear their acclamations of joy and gladness, embracing their once lost but now living brother. What heart would not melt at the sight of such a joyful scene? And what can I say to express my own feelings on this delightful interview? Having endured the hardships of an Indian captivity and the pains of the prison, the gnawings of hunger, the tortures of the rack, and the still more dreadful distress of twenty-two days' wandering in the wilderness; filled with despair, anxiety, and fear; almost starved, and nearly naked; full of wounds, and constantly chilled with the cold; imagine, kind reader, the feelings of my heart when I came to behold the face of affectionate parents and receive the tender embraces of beloved brothers and a loving sister. Think of the festivities of that evening, when I could again enjoy a seat in a social circle of friends and acquaintance around the fireside in my father's house.

Vain is the attempt to describe my own feelings on that joyful occasion. Fruitless indeed must be all my endeavors to express the mutual congratulations manifested by all on my return.

My long absence from my friends, together with a sense of the numerous and awful dangers through which I had been preserved, increased our gratitude, and caused wonder and astonishment to dwell in every breast. We could now heartily unite in ascribing praise and adoration to Him who granted me protection while exposed to the shafts of hatred and revenge. I was treated with all that friendship which pity could excite or sympathy dictate, and saluted by every person I met, whether old or young, with a hearty welcome. Every one seemed to be in a good degree conscious of the extreme sufferings I had undergone. In short, my return afforded me an opportunity to witness a display of all the tender passions of the soul.

Knowing the deplorable wretchedness of those who had the misfortune to become prisoners to the British, and consequently expecting every day to hear of my death, my friends were little less astonished at my return than they would have been had they witnessed the resurrection of one from the dead.

The extreme hunger and distress I had felt were clearly manifested to those who beheld my emaciated countenance and mangled feet; and no one was disposed to doubt the truth of my words who heard me relate the affecting tale of my sore afflictions. For, "by reason of the voice of my groanings, my bones," it might verily be said, did "cleave to my skin." I however had the satisfaction to find my deep anxiety to be delivered from bondage and escape from the enemy, my ardent wishes to see my friends, and my hungry, craving appetite, wholly satisfied in the full fruition of all my toils. The munificence of the wealthy was offered for my relief, and the poor approached me with looks of tenderness and pity. All things around me wore a propitious smile. From morning till night, instead of being guarded by a company of refugees and tories, or wandering in a lonesome wilderness, hungry and destitute, I could now behold the face of friends, and at the approach of night repose my head upon a downy pillow, under the hospitable covert of my father's roof.

Instead of being made a companion of the wretched, I could now enjoy the sweet conversation of a beloved sister and affectionate brothers.

Having for more than two years been deprived of hearing the gospel sound, surely "I was glad when they said unto me, Let us go into the house of the Lord." For unto God I could say, "Thou art my hiding-place; thou shalt preserve me from trouble; thou shalt compass me about with songs of deliverance. I will be glad and rejoice in thy name; for thou hast considered my trouble; thou hast known my soul in adversity." This I hoped would be the language of every one who made their escape with me. For myself, I trust it was the sincere language of my heart.

Notwithstanding the prisoners whom we left on the island were set at liberty shortly after our escape, and although our sufferings in the wilderness were exceedingly great, yet I never found cause to lament that I improved the opportunity to free myself from the hands of those cruel tormentors and oppressors of the afflicted. For "the spirit of a man will sustain his infirmity." And under this consideration we chose rather to hazard the consequences of an escape, though it might prove our death, than to become the menial servants, and thus gratify the infernal desires, of a petty tyrant.

> "Now I feel, by proof,
> That fellowship in pain divides not smart,
> Nor lightens aught each man's peculiar load."

I have never had the satisfaction to hear from either of my friends and fellow-sufferers, Clark and Sprague, since I parted with them at Bennington.

Mr. Belknap now lives in Randolph, Vermont, and, from the sad experience of the like sufferings himself and his participation in my own, can witness to the truth of my statement.

Let not the preservation of my life through such a train of dangers be attributed to mere chance; but let the praise be given to "God our Rock, and the high God our Redeemer."

In September, previous to my escape, a treaty of peace was concluded between Great Britain and the United States at Paris, the glad news of which reached America not long after my return, which occasioned the release of the remainder of the prisoners who were confined upon Prison Island.

As the war had now terminated, my return to Randolph would not be attended with the danger of being again made captive by the Indians;

which induced me, the spring following, to go to that place and resume my settlement.

On my arrival there I found my house was demolished, which recalled to mind the confusion and horror of that dreadful morning when the savage tribe approached, with awful aspect, my lonely dwelling. I went to work and erected a house upon the same spot, into which my father shortly after moved his family. The grass seed which the Indians had scattered for some distance from the house, as before observed, had taken root, stocked the ground, and remained entire for many years a fresh memento of that woful event, which proved but a faint prelude of all my direful sufferings.

Here my father lived by cultivating that soil which had borne the brutal band to my unwelcome door till April, 1812, when he died at the good old age of seventy-six. Here he has spent many a winter's evening in rehearsing the mournful tale of my "captivity and sufferings" to his friends and acquaintance.

Generous and hospitable by nature, and having been taught by my sufferings to feel for the needy, he was ever ready to extend the hand of charity to relieve their distresses. His house, always the abode of plenty, was an asylum for the naked and forlorn, an acceptable home to the poor and the wretched.

Always exhibiting a sense of what sufferings I had undergone for want of food, he seemed in nothing to be more delighted than "to feed the hungry and clothe the naked." My loving and aged step-mother, with one of her sons, (a half-brother of mine,) now lives on the same farm.

In the winter of 1785 I was married to Hannah Shurtliff, of Tolland, Connecticut, and settled at Randolph not far from my father's house, where I resided eight years, when I purchased a farm and removed to Brookfield, a town adjoining.

Here I have resided until the present time, (1816,) and obtained my own subsistence and that of my numerous family by means of cultivating the soil. By a steady course of industry and economy I have been enabled, under the divine blessing, to acquire a comfortable support, and enjoy the fruits of my labors in quietude and peace. As my occupation was that of a farmer, my opportunities for information, like those of many others of my class, have been limited.

My family, not unlike Job's, consists of seven sons and three daughters; nor have I reason to think my afflictions much inferior to his. Although death has never been permitted to enter my dwelling and take any of my family, yet my substance has once been destroyed by worse than Chaldean hands, and that, too, at the very outset of my adventures in life. Not only were my house and effects destroyed, but myself, at a most unpropitious hour, when far removed from all my friends, compelled to leave my employment, relinquish all those objects of enterprise peculiar to the juvenile age, and forced to enter the ranks of a savage band and travel into an enemy's country. Thus were all my expectations cut off. My hopes were blasted and my youthful prospects darkened. "I was not in safety, neither had I rest, neither was I quiet; yet trouble came. O that my grief were thoroughly weighed, and my calamity laid in the balances together!"

Notwithstanding that inhumanity and cruelty which characterized the conduct of the savages, yet I think that the barbarous treatment which we received from the impious commanders of the British fort, in whose charge we were kept, might put to the blush the rudest savage who traverses the western wild. Their conduct illy comported with what might be expected from men who are favored with the light of revelation.

The savage, when he does a deed of charity towards his prisoner, is no doubt less liable to be actuated by a selfish principle, and influenced by the hope of reward or by a fear of losing his reputation, than he is who has been made acquainted with the gracious reward offered to those who "do unto others as they would that others should do unto them," and knows the bitter consequences of the contrary practice.

And I think the destruction of Royalton and all its evil consequences may with less propriety be attributed to the brutal malevolence of the savage tribe than to the ignoble treachery and despicable fanaticism of certain individuals of our own nation.

Scarce can that man be found in this enlightened country who would treat his enemy with as much tenderness and compassion as I was treated by the savage tribe; though I had abundant cause to say that the "tender mercies of the wicked are cruel."

Who would not shudder at the idea of being compelled to take up their abode with a herd of tawny savages? Yet, alas! when I contrasted the sufferings I endured while with the Indians with those afflictions that were laid upon me by men who had been from their youth favored with the advantages of civilization, clothed with authority, and distinguished with a badge of honor, I could truly say the former chastised me with whips, but the latter with scorpions.

An Indian captivity will hardly admit of a comparison with my wretched condition while in the hands of the British and under the domineering power of a company of refugees and tories.

While with the Indians my food was unsavory and unwholesome; my clothing, like their own, was scant and covered with filthy vermin; and my life was always exposed to the danger of their implacable hatred and revenge. This was a most perilous condition indeed for any one to be placed in. But my confinement with the British multiplied my complaints, added to my afflictions, rendered me more exposed to the danger of losing my life, increased my sorrows, and apparently brought me near the grave. My food was less filthy; but I was not allowed the half of what my appetite craved and my nature required to render me comfortable.

By these and my subsequent afflictions I have been taught a lesson that has made an impression upon my mind which I trust will remain as long as life shall last.

I have been taught, by ocular demonstration and sad experience, the depravity of man, and the fallacy of looking for durable happiness in terrestrial things.

My own sufferings have implanted within my breast that sympathy for the distressed which is better felt than described. Nakedness and poverty have once been my companions; and I shall not readily forget to lend a listening ear to the cries of the needy.

And I would exhort myself and all my fellow-men, by the extreme sufferings I have endured, to be ready at all times to "feed the hungry and clothe the naked," nor ever fail to extend the hand of charity for the assistance of the unfortunate.

Names of a Part of the Persons killed and taken at the Burning of Royalton

Zadock Steele, taken at Randolph
Experience Davis
Elias Curtis
J. Parks
Moses Parsons
Simeon Belknap, now living in Randolph
Samuel Pember
Thomas Pember, killed at Royalton
Gardner Rix, now living at Royalton
Daniel Downer
Joseph Kneeland, killed at the encampment at Randolph
Jonathan Brown, now residing in Williamstown
Adan Durkee, died at Montreal
Joseph Havens
Peter Hutchinson

John Hutchinson, now living in Bethel
———— Avery
John Kent
Peter Mason
Giles Gibbs, killed at Randolph
Elias Button, killed at Royalton
Nathaniel Gilbert

*The following Persons were released by the
Intercession of Mrs. Hendee*

Daniel Downer, Jr.
Andrew Durkee
Michael Hendee
Roswell Parkhurst
Shelden Durkee
Joseph Rix
Rufus Fish
———— Fish
Nathaniel Evans

[from *Indian Narratives: Containing a Correct and Interesting History of the Indian Wars, from the Landing of Our Pilgrim Fathers, 1620 to Gen. Wayne's Victory, 1794* (Claremont, N.H.: Tracy and Brothers, 1854), 209–76.]

GEORGE AVERY

—◦❯❯•❮❮◦—

George Avery, another captive taken during the British-Indian raid on the Roy-
alton area, also left an account of his experiences. While nowhere as complete
an account as that of Zadock Steele, Avery's journal contains interesting infor-
mation on both captives and captors, and illustrates the enduring theme of the
captivity as an experience for moral education, and the captivity narrative as a
form of confessional literature. Printed here with minimal alteration from the
original, it is published for the first time, courtesy of Dartmouth College.

George Avery's Journal of the Royalton Raid

A BRIEF SKETCH of some of author of the foregoing treatises experience and tryals in life.

When young, I was taught strictly to obey the forms of religion. I had
many tryals by conviction of sin, and of its deserts. Taught by parents,
who was strictly observers. I was taught to pray and used the formal
way of praying and tryed in a measure to live up to it, but often came
short of even the form of it. I neither knew nor was I taught much of
the corruption of the heart. and the neede of a change in the mind and
affections I sometimes statedly for sometime together, and again neglected untill some awakenings of concience—and again forgitting duties I passed time in a neglegt way, while I arrived to manhood. I was
21 years old Jan 23d day AD1780 I had left my parents care and theire
good rules and admonitions; I was an unsteady youth and leaving strict
discipline seemed to be set more at liberty from its yoke, This was in
the time of the revolutionary war that seperated the American provinces
from Great Britan, I was a soldier stationed at Milford Connecticut that
winter. The next summer, in August I was in Sharon, Vt. clearing land
intending to be a farmer, A giddy youth with vain expectations to be
something in the world. I comepare my self to the words of the poet.
Through all the follies of the mind; he smells and snufs [?] the emty
wind.

I was too regardless of the sabbath, lived a careless loose life with
other young comerads of the same cast which I resided with, occupied
in the same way. One Sabbath forgitting the day of the week, we wear

at work, at husking corn, an old lady passed by us with solemn countenance agoing to meeting. She never chid us, but I began to think there
was some thing wrong, and told my mates, I guissed it was Sabbath day,
Why they replyed, My reply was, The old lady had on her Sabbathday
mouth! it was my rudeness altho I had strong convictions of our carelessness forgitting the Sabbath. I felt no so light as I made to appear. It
was not the way I was brought up, which caused some reflections of my
past conduct, and brought tears to my eyes. We left our work for that
Sabbath. That night following I slept with my comerads on the floar of
the shantee. I dreamed I was beset by serpents the most hidious and
numerous that I ever saw, and awoke in the horrible fright. but my fears
soone vanished, and I was soone a sleepe again, and dreamed of being
besett by Indians and as frightfully awakened as before. But haveing no
faith in dreams, my fears soone vanished, it was now broadday light.
That morning I wen to a neighbour for our bread, while my mates
cooked breakfast. When I returned I met my companions affrighted run-
ing to the woods, but I did not apprehend so much danger as they did
from Indians, I thought of going to the camp and save my cloaths. I
made light of it and told them I would git my breakfast first—I went
and got my cloaths and hid them, I but tasted the breakfast. I saw others
flying for safety, and spoke to one, He said some had turned to go and
fight and the Indians I thought of going a very short distance from us
and I should know if they had. But turning a few rods I was surprised
by the sight of two Indians very near me. The foremost one with to-
mohok in hand we were face to face suddenly both stopped. He waved
his hand Come, come. I answered the Indian come and took to my heeles
and ran for escape followed the road on the river bank but a little jumped
in to the bushes on its bank out of his sight and made for foarding the
river the two followed me the tommahok one caught me in the back of
the collar of my cloaths and gave me a few blows with his instrument
and a few greeting words How How (that is Run Run) There I was as
really affrighted as I was in my dreams but a few hours before (But the
dreams did not here occure to my mind) The two Indians stripped one
of my outside garments I being lame, at that time. They took me by each
arm and I ran betwene them, to return to theire company which they
left that were destroying houses and cattle and had taken other prisoners.
They had killed two of the inhabitants in pursuing them vis. Pember and
Button. They spent the chief part of the day in burning and killing property. The night they encamped near the place of theire destruction. This
first encampment was in Randolph Woods the 16 of Oct 1780. About
350 Indians and 26 prisoners. The Indians made fiers and shelters of

Hemlock boughs to encamp by for the night as many as 20 or more. The prisoners had different masters at different camps. The prisoners were striped of outer garments by their masters and collected at the Chiefs officers encampment. We stood huddled together the fier betwene us and the officer. An Indian came to a prisoner took him by the hand to lead him off. The head officer told the prisoner to go with him and bid farewell. A prisoner near by me whispers me, I believe he will in another world. I asked why. He replied he had contenantal cloaths and was a soldier when taken. By this I was frightened. Then others were led off in the same way. I think my turn might be about the 6 or 7th. Judge reader my feelings if you can, for I am not able to express them in any other way but by confusion in thoughts, like one to die violently. I expect I became quite fantick, When I was led a short distance through woods to the camp where the Indians were cooking all looked calm and peaceble to my view and astonishment. The silly phantick thought struck my mind. They'll fat me before they kill me. Soone however they brought a strong belt to bind me aimed it at my body (to put it arround me,) then took me to a booth (or shelter). I was laid down under it feete to the fier Stakes drove down in the ground each side of me my belt tied to them stakes. Thus I was staked to the ground: To look up there was a long Indian knives fastned to the boughs, This condition looked fright-full but I had gon through the greatest, Still here is no safety. They gave me here of their supper but I cannot tell the relish of it that night, after supper 4 Indians lay on my belt that tied me to the stakes two upon each side of me so that I could not move but that they all would feele the belt move. When I looked at the fier there was the guard an Indian smoking. In the morning the Vermont Milisha routed them. They fired on the Indian but guard. The Indians in confusion and rage unstaked theire prisoners. My belt was taken and put round my neck and tied to a sapplin another I see bound to a tree while they packed up. Theire eyes looked like wildfier, one uttered to his prisoner bumby bumby (as tho death at hand) After ready to march I was loosed from the sapplin loaded with a pack and led by the halter on my neck and my leader with tommahok in hand and to follow after my file leader.

Each master of a prisoner (as I understood afterward) had orders to kill his prisoner if closely pursued and then they could take theire flight from their enemies in the woods. In this case no one could predict the result, life and death is set before us. There must follow a multitude of Thoughts which none can know but by experiance. Many vain wishes I had in this unreconsciled state. Oh that I were nothing so that they could not torment my body. Then again, Why is it thus with me, is the

reasonable enquiry. (It seemed according to the circumstance, when I
was taken I might have got out of the way). Now my dreams rushed to
mind, This made me feele that there was an over ruling providence. I
immediately felt I had to doo with my maker God. I felt in His hand
aguilty sinner. I compared myself like unto a bullock unaccustomed to
the yoak, such feelings I never had before in my life brought to my view
my sins roled over me like the waves of the sea, roling after each other
untill I was overwhelmed, it seemed He told me all I ever did. I felt the
evill of my life, and the Divine Justice of providence. I was still as to a
murmor against God. I was soone calmed in mind. I saw they wear
overrulled by God, the Indians, could do no more than they were permitted to doo, they could do no more than a Wise and good disposer
pleased I seemed to feele that calmness to think that if they were the
Indians permitted to kill I could look them in the face calmly. The words
in Isaiah came to mind. He was led as a sheap to the slaughter and as
a lamb dumb before his shearers was dumb so opened he not his mouth.
As I was litterally so led. I have thought in my tryals since it might be
the occasion of these blessed words of comeing to mind. My mind in
this tryal was calm I was silent as to a murmer. I opened not my mouth.
My soul was stilled it was God that did it. But whoo can give peace,
and still the murmor of an unreconciled mind, but God; under such
tryals of mind and providence?

(But I have enough to complain of my self as a sinner against Divine
goodnes which provokes chastisement).

I had at this time the Holy Bible and Watses Hymn Book in my boo-
som, that we used to read and meditate in our Journy, which I took
from a house that the Indians burned. The Indians would take them
from my bosom to see what I had got and return them. In one of our
stops, in reading the 88th psalm as applicable in part to our case it drew
many tears from sum of us. These books was read by us on our journey
to Cannada and consoling to us when prisoners. We had no where to
look but to God in our troubles. But as sinners we have still that body
of sin that provokes chastisement and causes grief to the soul which we
hope will mortify the deeds of the Body to die unto sin to live unto God.

But never having ben taught or to hear of any one tell an experience
or exersises of a change of mind or the new birth or have any encouragement by understanding Christians I knew not to call my exercises
Christian experience.

Alltho I had lived under the stated means of Grace I had never heard
any one tell a Christian experience when taken into church felloship or
any tryals of the christian mind Altho unacquainted with such advan-

tages and priviledges, yeat I remember my own feelings and exersises of mind and the Goodness of God under such tryals. I have degressed from the Historical part of my work. To show the exersises of the mind in such tryals and the Goodness of God in them is more than I can express I now return to the Indian history; I traveled with them 5 days. Taken by them on Monday Oct 16th we came to Lake Shamplan on Friday 20th at Colchester and crossed over in Battows to the Grand Ile that day. (They had killed two of the inhabitats in persuing to take them vis— Button and Pember. Also in the camp the first night they killed two of theire prisoners vis. Kneland and Gibs.) Nothing further transpired thus far that is very intresting to relate. We went down the Lake from the Grand Ile, to the Ile o Noix Saterday 21st, tarried there that night for refreshment by victuals & rum. Sabbath 22 we arrived at St Johns Cannaday, where was more rum, that day and a market for theire plunder. I was dressed drolely I had on an Indian blanket with my head polked through a hole in its middle, hanging over my body, with a high peaked cap on my head, my face painted with read streaks, being smoked over their fires looked very much like an Indian, being sett at a parsel of their plundered goods. The refugees at St. Johns came to the parsel that I was sat at, to buy, looking at me one of them says to his mate, is that an Indian; his mate replies, no, his hair is not Indian. (Thus look and see Indian captives). The Indians this day (sabbath) take up thier march for theire home Cohnawagoga, many of them very drunk and often those loaded down with theire plundered goods would soused down in mud as road was much soaked by the snows melting at that time. Some of those loaded drunken Indians in this plight were three days traviling 25 miles. I was taken by my Master Indian to Cahnawoga at his home we arrived on Monday or Tuesday St Johns. I tarried there at my keepers two or more days when all the party or the scout of Indians came in. The Sachem Tommo [?] came to my quarters, and tooke me when fired with wampum and neatly painted up. He took me to the centre of Village, where the Indians and Squaws gathered arround I was on a seat at the Chiefs feet, He making a speach over me to his audience, I sat in suspence, (not knowing his language) or designs I had fears as might be to run the gauntlet or some evill. But my suspence soone ended. I was led off by an Indian lad bye past the Spectators to the doar of a house and meet by Squaws with a blanket and hat, and water and soap to wash; and found that was the place of my residence. Theire I found another young man a prisoner to them I inquired of him if he understood the meaning of this last manover I had passed through, He said he did, He had experienced the same. We were both of us, (by this seremony)

adopted into that family to fill the places of two Indians which had recently died there and we made up theire loss. I enquired of him how he
know, He answered the Indian interpreter Tracy told him. But what I
saw afterward which was more affecting, that they displayed the scalps
of our prisoners (those they killed) in the same seremony. I lived with
them something 6 or 7 weeks perhaps until my owner belonging to another tribe came for me, and took me to Montreale to take his bounty
for me I was dressed descently to follow him by two old squaws; as soon
as I was told and Delivered to the Brittish a prisoner I was stripped to
the shirt by my former Indian owner—I was taken thence to the guard
house allmost naked they covered me with an old thin blanket coat in
the cold season of the last of Novr–keept under guard naught to eat for
2 or more days before I hand orders for rat [?] from thence I was taken
to grants Iland near the City a Rany night followed the prisoners was
in tents there in cold winter weather. We prisoners had no tent pitched
for the night we roled ourselves in the tent cloth for a cold wet night. I
never drew rations on the Island I complained to the officer of prisoners
of lameness, and carried from thence to the Hospital half starved the
next day, being shifted without orders for provisions (from place to
place) I was almost starved. I was lame when I was taken with a scor-
fioulous tumor in my legg. A surgeon and phisian tended the Hospital
they were kind to me, especially the Doctor. When I got better of the
sore leg the phicisian ment to take me to his House to serve him. I was
both very dirty and naked—from thence I was conducted in such a
plight in a cold winters day to the commisary (by the orderly man of
the hospital) for cloathing, and got none from there to the Doctors. left
there for the night chilled with cold fatigued and sick—hardly able to
rise next morning I was called upon by the Doctor examined by Him
and sent back to the Hospital, a mile to travill in a cold N Wester I went
directly there and took my place in the Bunk; I was soone senceless of
all that passed. The time was lost to me, for a space and deranged views
and thoughts followed. When I had come to reason or sense of feeling
I had accute pain in the head my eyes seemed as if they be thumped
out.* [*In this case the Doctor ordered half of my head shaved the left
side three blister plasters were applied on my head neck and back that
on head and neck never blistered—and the back one scarce a blister.]
When I had got to know my self I was amasiated to a Skillet. When I
got cloaths to put on my overalls, I looked like tongs in them my ear to
see through my nose and face peaked [?] and dirty and lowsy as if one
did all as they lay in the bunk. I used to bake the rags of my shirt on
the stove [?] when I had got so much strength, better to keep lice off.

Through the mercy of God I recovered from this distress; and when
better of it, I was amasiated to a scelaton in putting on pants looked like
putting tongs in them. face peeked and ears thin to see through, and in
recovering in this weak condition I had to take prisoners hard fare I have
had to leave the Hospital for the bunkhouse [?] when so weak as to fall
in the snow and crawl and clamber up by things to git into the hous
again. I write now what was done about 65 years ago in the year 1781
Feby. Now July 20 1846. And now what shal I render to the Lord for
His astonishing goodness I will take the cup & what stupid hardness
must it bee not to notice the Divine hand. The Doctor still showing his
kindness to me, (he did not need me as a waiter to himself) but he saught
for places for my abode where I was needed, (to my relief from confinement). He had two places in view for me, one was to live with a Jew
in Montreal, the other, to live with a Jew at Barkey (as I might choose).
This Jew was a merchant 45 miles distant; I put it to the Doctor to
choose for me, He thought it best to go to Berkey in the country a way
from the City. The refugees often quarraled and complined of the prisoners at liberty in the city and got them into prison again. I went by his
choice. The Jew was a country trader with but very little lerning, but of
strong memory and head trained [?] to cast up accounts without the use
of figures or writing, He had and did employ french men to make up
his accounts. Very shortly after I went there I keept his accounts. (When
the Doctor chose this place for me to live I told him I should loose of
being exchanged being so far from other prisoners; or of writing to my
parents; he answered that could be accommodated, by writing to Mr.
Jones the provost master of Montreall.) When I went to live with the
Jew my clothing was but poor an old blanket loose coat, the rag of a
shirt that I burned the lice from and overalls that I can describe (I drew
allso a shirt with my overalls, and not a prisoner died and I had his old
shoes when I went with the Jew to live.) A shirt was the first I most
needed and the first thing I was supplied with from him, and that was
made from Orinbrigs (coars wrapping cloth) washed in cold water and
dried for me to put on by an Old matroon the Jews housekeeper. When
I put this shirt on, the meanest I ever wore except the old dirty lousy
ragged one, it daunted my Spirits; other wise I had better fare, and when
better acquainted he needed my assistance to keepe his accounts and in
his store. He married a wife soon after I went there to live, she was a
Jewes. His family before was the Old french woman & 2 twin children
he had by a Squaw, when a trader with the Indians which he was obliged
to leave in upper Cannada. But after he married I faired better for cloathing by her means I was dressed descent. I tarried with them untill the

next August. The Jew left home for Quebeck while gone I wrote to Mr.
Jones informing him where I was, and to know if theire was any exchange of prisoners, or that I could write to my parents. I wanted the
benefit of it. Mr. Jones wrote immediately to the Jew to send me to
Montreall, and there I was exchanged and to be sent home. This letter
came, when Mr. Lions the Jew returned from Quebeck and I was absent
from home, on an arrand. When I returned in the evening, the Jew enquired of me what I had ben about while he was gone to Quebeck. Why
I answered. He responded I have received a letter from Mr. Jones at
Montreall and I don't know what they are a going to do with you it may
be to put you to jaile. (He could not read the letter at all, neither his wife
so as to understand it.) He wanted me to read it to them. I took it and
looked it through, and then read to them, gladly, that I was exchanged
to go home and that he must send me directly to Montreall. Then says
he what shall we do, for you have keept my books while here. You and
Mrs. Lyons must set up all night and she must write over the head of
every mans account his name in Hebrew characters for she did not know
how to write english or french well enough, and we spent the night in
this way.

The next morning I set out for Montreall arrived there the next day,
when I came to Mr. Jones' I was told I might have been at home by this
time, that I was exchanged by name and 17 others and that they had
gone in a carteel [?] home and that I had to wait there untill another
carteele of prisoners might go. He told me I could draw provisions (and
have my liberty) and be bilited with prisoners that were on parrole untill
I could go, so I lived with others drew my provisions weakly and worke
out as I pleased I thus employed my self to gain something to cloth and
to spare to the poor sick prisoners, in the hospital that I before suffered
in. The next June a carteele of prisoners came into the state, and I with
the next, and was landed at the head of the Lake Shamplane, at what is
now Whitehall, N. York. From thence I traveled on foot to Windsor
Connecticut to my Sisters and was gladly and surprisingly welcomed for
they knew nothing but that I were dead and scalped untill they saw me
(for by mistak my name had been returned, and published as dead) I
tarried at Windsor through that summer, and wrote to my parents in
Truro Mass. I worked and bought me hors to go home; on the first of
Sept following I sett out for Truro and arrived in the neighbourhood of
my fathers; and sent a neighbour to notify my parents that I was come,
that theire lost had arrived, not too shock them too suddenly. My mother
and sister had gathered themselves in a roome to mete me, Soone I met
them in that roome, at the sight of me my mother left the roome, Judg

Reader if you can of her emotions off mind and ours. I feele the emotions now when writing. My father was absent from home at this time, but had learned of my arrival before he came home that evening with his mind more composed.

["George Avery's Journal of the Royalton Raid," photocopy in Dartmouth College Special Collections, Ms. 780900.6, printed by permission of Dartmouth College Library.]

Suggestions for Further Reading

Axtell, James. *The European and the Indian: Essays in the Ethnohistory of Co-lonial America* (New York: Oxford University Press, 1981).
————. *The Invasion Within: The Contest of Cultures in Colonial North Amer-ica* (New York: Oxford University Press, 1985).
————. "The White Indians of Colonial America," *William and Mary Quar-terly,* 3d series, 32 (1975), 55–88.
Baker, C. Alice. *True Stories of New England Captives Carried to Canada Dur-ing the Old French and Indian Wars* (Cambridge, Mass.: A. E. Hall, 1897).
Calloway, Colin G. *Dawnland Encounters: Indians and Europeans in Northern New England* (Hanover, N.H.: University Press of New England, 1991).
————. "An Uncertain Destiny: Indian Captivities on the Upper Connecticut River," *Journal of American Studies* 17 (1983), 189–210.
————. *The Western Abenakis of Vermont, 1600–1800: War, Migration, and the Survival of an Indian People* (Norman: University of Oklahoma Press, 1990).
Chase, Francis, ed., *Gathered Sketches from the Early History of New Hamp-shire and Vermont* (Claremont, N.H.: Tracy, Kenney and Co., 1856; re-printed Heritage Books, Inc., 1987).
Coleman, Emma Lewis, *New England Captives Carried to Canada Between 1677 and 1760 During the French and Indian Wars,* 2 vols. (Portland, Maine: The Southworth Press, 1925).
Drake, Samuel G., ed., *Indian Captivities, or Life in the Wigwam* (Auburn, Mass.: Derby and Miller, 1852).
Haviland, William A., and Marjory W. Power, *The Original Vermonters: Native Inhabitants, Past and Present* (Hanover, N.H.: University Press of New England, 1981).
Heard, Norman. *White into Red: A Study of the Assimilation of White Persons Captured by Indians* (Metuchen, N.J.: Scarecrow Press, 1973).
Slotkin, Richard, *Regeneration Through Violence: The Mythology of the Amer-ican Frontier, 1600–1860* (Middletown, Conn.: Wesleyan University Press, 1974).
Smith, Robinson V. "New Hampshire Persons Taken as Captives by the Indi-ans," *Historical New Hampshire* 8 (October 1952), 24–31.
Ulrich, Laurel Thatcher, *Good Wives: Image and Reality in the Lives of Women in Northern New England, 1650–1750* (New York: Knopf, 1982).
Vaughan, Alden T., and Edward W. Clark, eds., *Puritans among the Indians: Accounts of Captivity and Redemption 1676–1724* (Cambridge, Mass.: The Belknap Press of Harvard University Press, 1981).

Vaughan, Alden T., and Daniel Richter, "Crossing the Cultural Divide: Indians and New Englanders, 1605–1765," *Proceedings of the American Antiquarian Society* 90 (1980), 23–99.
Washburn, Wilcomb E., comp., *Narratives of North American Captivities,* 111 vols. (New York: Garland Publishing, Inc., 19—).

CPSIA information can be obtained
at www.ICGtesting.com
Printed in the USA
BVOW08s1303261017
498702BV00001B/2/P